Celtic Shamanism

The Ultimate Guide to Celtic Druidry, Spirituality, Earth Magic, Spells, Symbols, and Tree Astrology

© Copyright 2023 - All rights reserved.

The content contained within this book may not be reproduced, duplicated, or transmitted without direct written permission from the author or the publisher.

Under no circumstances will any blame or legal responsibility be held against the publisher, or author, for any damages, reparation, or monetary loss due to the information contained within this book, either directly or indirectly.

Legal Notice:

This book is copyright protected. It is only for personal use. You cannot amend, distribute, sell, use, quote, or paraphrase any part, or the content within this book, without the consent of the author or publisher.

Disclaimer Notice:

Please note the information contained within this document is for educational and entertainment purposes only. All effort has been executed to present accurate, up-to-date, reliable, and complete information. No warranties of any kind are declared or implied. Readers acknowledge that the author is not engaging in the rendering of legal, financial, medical, or professional advice. The content within this book has been derived from various sources. Please consult a licensed professional before attempting any techniques outlined in this book.

By reading this document, the reader agrees that under no circumstances is the author responsible for any losses, direct or indirect, that are incurred as a result of the use of the information contained within this document, including, but not limited to, errors, omissions, or inaccuracies.

Free Bonus from Silvia Hill available for limited time

Hi Spirituality Lovers!

My name is Silvia Hill, and first off, I want to THANK YOU for reading my book.

Now you have a chance to join my exclusive spirituality email list so you can get the ebooks below for free as well as the potential to get more spirituality ebooks for free! Simply click the link below to join.

P.S. Remember that it's 100% free to join the list.

~~$27~~ FREE BONUSES

9 Types of Spirit Guides and How to Connect to Them

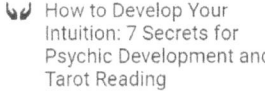
How to Develop Your Intuition: 7 Secrets for Psychic Development and Tarot Reading

Tarot Reading Secrets for Love, Career, and General Messages

Access your free bonuses here
https://livetolearn.lpages.co/celtic-shamanism-paperback/

Table of Contents

INTRODUCTION 1
CHAPTER 1: THE ROOTS OF SHAMANISM 3
CHAPTER 2: WHAT IS A CELTIC SHAMAN? 13
CHAPTER 3: WHO ARE THE DRUIDS? 19
CHAPTER 4: CELTIC DEITIES AND SYMBOLS 27
CHAPTER 5: OGHAM: THE CELTIC TREE ALPHABET 40
CHAPTER 6: DRUIDIC TREE ASTROLOGY 50
CHAPTER 7: CELTIC ANIMAL MAGIC 76
CHAPTER 8: EARTH MAGIC RITUALS 81
CHAPTER 9: CELTIC SPELLS AND CHARMS 92
CHAPTER 10: CELTIC HOLIDAYS AND FESTIVALS 98
APPENDIX: GLOSSARY OF GAELIC TERMS 103
HERE'S ANOTHER BOOK BY SILVIA HILL THAT YOU MIGHT LIKE ... 106
FREE BONUS FROM SILVIA HILL AVAILABLE FOR LIMITED TIME 107
REFERENCES 108

Introduction

The Celtic people are one of the oldest cultures in the British Isles. Much of it survives to this day through the modern cultures of those living in Ireland, Scotland, Wales, and parts of England. The Gaelic, Cornish, Welsh, Breton, Manx, and Scottish Gaelic languages are all considered part of the Celtic family of languages, having evolved from the original Proto-Celtic language spoken by the ancient Celts. Their influence can be felt even beyond these languages - many of the customs, festivals, holidays, and religious practices of the people living in the British Isles can be directly linked back to the ancient Celtic culture.

The fascination many people have with the Celtic people stems from the way society developed from the classical to late medieval eras of history. This was a transitional period, as the native Celtic and Anglo-Saxon tribes living in the British Isles were first exposed to Continental European cultures through the invasion, conquest, and occupation carried out by the Roman Empire. Once they arrived, Christianity followed not long after. The strife between the Celtic and Roman people caused a significant shift in the characteristics of both cultures.

While Christianity became increasingly prominent, it became a standard procedure for missionaries to work toward assimilating the local populace with as little resistance as possible. They used this tactic in an attempt to adapt the deities, myths, and religious practices of the native peoples into existing Christian dogma. This process is known as syncretization, where the Christian angels, saints, and feast days are assigned an association with similar parts of the local religion. However, it wasn't a one-way street. Celtic paganism also adopted pieces of Christianity into their own belief system.

One of the few irreconcilable aspects of Celtic culture that Christianity refused to acknowledge were the roles of certain religious leaders, like shamans and Druids. Although superficially similar to priests, bishops, and cardinals, their practices and beliefs were incongruent with Christianity's viewpoint on souls, spirits, and magic. Shamans and Druids became increasingly irrelevant, becoming victims of Christian assimilation. For centuries afterward, they were effectively extinct, with only a few pockets of surviving Celtic pagans still possessing either one.

Fortunately, the neopagan revival and reconstruction of the ancient Celtic religion included the resurrection of shamans and Druids as respectable spiritual occupations. Their emphasis on preserving nature and encouraging people to live in harmony with existing ecosystems has become much more relevant as the subject of environmentalism is pushed to the forefront of societal responsibilities. Shamans and Druids set a positive example of how we can utilize natural resources without harming the environment. If their warnings are not heeded, there might not be much of a world left for future generations to inherit.

With thousands of years' worth of history behind it, the Celtic religion and culture is a very appealing subject to explore. Many aspects of Celtic society can teach you lessons applicable to the current age. When you start reading this guide, keep that fact in mind, and try to look at it through the lens of a 21st-century audience. Some parts of the ancient Celtic culture might seem far removed from the modern experience, but we have more in common with our ancestors than you might initially believe. If you immerse yourself in everything surrounding Celtic traditions, you will emerge with a much greater understanding of a people who can live harmoniously alongside nature without causing irreparable harm.

Chapter 1: The Roots of Shamanism

Shamanism is a religious practice involving mysticism and animism, with a heavy focus on the spiritual realm. Its roots extend back thousands of years and across many different cultures. This included the Celtic and Gaelic people in Ireland and Scotland, Native Americans in North America, the indigenous peoples of South America, and other pockets of select tribal cultures in Asia and Australia. Each developed its own brand of shamanism, but they all had a few key components in common that made them recognizable as the same basic practice.

Shamanism is a religious practice involving mysticism and animism.
https://unsplash.com/photos/89tJEmx3VuA

Basic Aspects of Shamanism

The concept of the spiritual realm and the spirits that inhabit it are considered by shamanism to be an important part of an individual's experience, as well as having a role in society at large. Spirits can be benevolent, malevolent, or a combination of both. Finding ways to communicate with these spirits is one of the primary functions of shamans, who are believed to be able to enter the spiritual realm and treat illnesses caused by malevolent spirits. Benevolent spirits are often consulted by a shaman when seeking answers to questions outside their own breadth of knowledge.

Part of shamanism includes using animal symbols and imagery, as animals are seen as spirit guides that assist people in overcoming obstacles in their lives. Sometimes, these animals can also serve as messengers from the spiritual realm or provide omens to forewarn the shaman of major events to come. Shamans can perform divination rituals to more actively discern the future, use runes or bones, and scry for hints about things beyond their ken. Sometimes, they can even induce trances to enter a state of ecstasy where they have visions or undertake a vision quest.

Shamanistic Beliefs

Shamanism's main belief is that an invisible spiritual realm exists alongside the physical world, where spirits of a wide variety dwell. It also maintains that there is a spiritual power within all living beings. However, the potency of this power is stronger in certain beings, such as humans or sacred animals. Learning how to identify these spirits and connect to the spiritual realm can allow a shaman to gain knowledge and power they would not otherwise be accessible.

The Soul

The soul is essentially the spirit contained within a living being, particularly a human. This is the part that continues on after death and enters the spiritual realm. Some forms of shamanism even believe that a person can possess two or more souls simultaneously. In these cases, one of the souls will always remain with the person's body, known appropriately as the "body soul." The others can leave the body at will and are called the "wandering souls." A shaman must have at least two souls to perform their duties, as they are sometimes required to send their wandering soul away from their body to enter the spiritual realm and commune with the spirits living there.

The Spirits

The spirits associated with shamanism are often seen in the form of humans or animals. The soul is believed to leave the body, either consciously while alive or unconsciously after death, and the soul is then transported to the spiritual realm. Some animals are also considered spirits, even in their physical bodies, due to their strong connection to the spiritual realm. Animals like eagles, wolves, jaguars, snakes, and rats are viewed as spirit animals by many shamanistic traditions, and using their actions and behaviors can assist a shaman in reading omens and determining the future.

Animism

Animism is the belief that everything in nature has its own spiritual representations with which a shaman can interact. This includes animals, trees, flowers, and plants and the elemental forces of fire, earth, water, and air. As with most spirits, these have the potential to be both good and evil, and a shaman can communicate with them directly. It requires a strong foundational understanding of how the world works in relation to the spirits for a shaman to successfully navigate the spiritual realm.

The Spiritual Realm

The spiritual realm is considered a non-ordinary reality, meaning it is an entirely separate and distinct world from ordinary reality. The spirit realm exists in the same physical space as the real world but is hidden by a veil that can only be pierced by shamans and other exceptional individuals. This is where all spirits dwell when they no longer possess a physical form. Those trained to walk among the spirits may send their souls to the spiritual realm to communicate with the spirits that reside there. While people cannot normally see the spirits living within the spiritual realm, they can see those in the physical world, watching events and learning secrets that they can pass along to shamans.

Most traditions maintain that the spiritual realm is divided into three tiers, the lower, middle, and upper levels. A spirit's position within this hierarchy is dependent on the amount of spiritual power they possess, with the most important dwelling within the upper level, while the least important are constrained to the lower level. The spirits of dead humans are generally seen in the middle level, as the lower one is reserved for the majority of animal spirits, and the upper level is designated for the most enlightened beings.

Interconnectivity

The majority of shamans believe that everything is fundamentally interconnected. The physical world and the spiritual realm are enmeshed in a way that precludes one from operating normally without the other. Some of it is seen as having a give-and-take relationship between the spirits and the shamans. Suppose someone is attempting to catch fish for their family to survive. In that case, a shaman might beseech the spirits to allow the fisherman to catch what they need. In return, the spirits are compensated for this boon through prayers and sacrifices. It is a holistic approach to the universe's mechanics, thriving on this interconnectivity and equal exchange of favors.

Healing Powers

Most shamans can use their connection to the spirits to heal the body, the mind, and the soul. It is believed that when a person becomes sick, one of the causes may be that their soul has strayed from their physical body, so a shaman must retrieve the missing soul and reunite it with the ailing person. In other instances, a shaman can appeal to the spirits to use their energy to help encourage healing within an injured person, speeding up their recovery time. When someone is having problems with their mind or soul, shamans can also communicate with the spirits to get advice on how to help them fix the person's troubles.

Fertility

Some shamanistic cultures believe that when a woman struggles with fertility issues, the cause may be due to the lack of a soul for the child she is trying to conceive. To remedy this situation, a shaman can visit the spiritual realm to locate the lost soul of the child and bring it back to their mother, thus solving the problem. Shamans also have the ability to ask the spirits about a potential future child, such as what their name should be or what their destiny could hold. When a woman is infertile and a shaman cannot find their child's soul, the shaman may be able to contact the spirits to discover why this has happened.

Hunting

When hunting game or other animals, there must be some sort of appeasement given to their souls when they are killed. This includes using shamans to communicate with the released souls of the animals and give them thanks for their sacrifice, as well as beseech them to speak to their living brethren, convincing them to allow themselves to be killed for the benefit of the hunter. As many shamanistic cultures view animals as both sacred and a source of food, they feel it is essential to ensure that they do not offend the spirits of the animals they slay. They make it clear that the killing is not made out of malice but out of necessity, which the animals usually understand.

The System of Shamanism

Shamanism has several different systems and practices that are included in their religion. To enter the spiritual realm, they must travel across the "axis mundi," or the hidden ley lines between the Earth's two poles. They bring about a state of extra-sensory consciousness by inducing an ecstatic trance, which can be achieved by ritual performances, autohypnosis - essentially hypnotizing themselves - or by using entheogens. Each shamanistic culture employs its own methods, but sometimes these practices can be used in conjunction.

Ritual Performances

The types of ritual performances a shaman can use to enter the spiritual realm often involve music and songs. Like the different forms of shamanism itself, the types of music and songs used are equally diverse. Sometimes, a shaman will imitate sounds from nature, including those made by animals, using onomatopoeias. They will put them in the form of a song, repeating certain significant sounds as a chorus to help them get into the state of mind to transcend their physical body. Other types of music and songs can be closer to those most people would find familiar, using instruments and traditional vocal singing, or even throat singing, as performed by many Inuit cultures. The purpose of these performances is to break free the shaman from the physical world, allowing their soul to enter the spiritual realm and commune with the spirits therein.

Autohypnosis

Autohypnosis is similar to meditation in that a person uses relaxation techniques and concentration of the mind to direct their thoughts and energy toward a specific goal. Shamans can do this as a means of entering the spiritual realm. They will separate themselves from all distractions and focus all their energy on sending their soul to commune with the spirits. When this is done successfully, a shaman can easily travel across the spiritual realm and gain insight and knowledge from those they meet. When they are finished, they can return to their body and snap themselves out of their hypnotic state.

Entheogens

An entheogen is a psychoactive substance (i.e., a drug) used to induce a heightened state of consciousness in which a shaman can cross over into the spiritual realm. Entheogen means "generating the divine within," so the idea is that through their use, a shaman is able to send their soul into the spiritual realm to connect with the spirits dwelling there. When used in a ritualistic context by experienced shamans, entheogens are not considered dangerous, as shamans have been trained to apply their effects safely. Entheogens can be substances like peyote, psilocybin mushrooms, uncured tobacco, salvia divinorum, iboga, cannabis, and ayahuasca. These are all-natural psychoactive substances. Synthetic drugs like LSD or ecstasy are not permitted for ritualistic purposes.

Shamanism around the World

Shamanism can be found in cultures worldwide, although each has its own variations that make them unique. Because it extends back so far in history, it is impossible to know whether shamanism began in one culture and spread to others through trade and war or if each brand of shamanism was developed independently. However, the fact that they all share common aspects speaks to the universal appeal of the religion, even in cultures that may look very different, as they all still hold to the belief of spirits and the spiritual realm existing alongside the physical world.

Africa

Shamanism in Africa can be found among the Dogon, the Sisala, the Zulu, the Nguni, and the Karanga people. Shamans are also often called "medicine men," and part of their duties include warding off evil spirits. Illnesses are thought to be the product of witchcraft, necessitating a shaman to counter the evil magic and heal the sick. Shamans can also be herbalists; they are needed to help maintain a balance within nature and keep people from suffering from the negative effects of disharmony between the living and the dead.

Asia

The Hmong people in China had professional shamans who used rituals and trances to bring harmony to individuals, families, and communities, preventing the environment from becoming hostile to them. In Japan, the Shinto and Ainu religions include shamanism, especially Shinto, which promotes shamans as a major part of their agricultural societies. North and South Korea have shamans, although the male shamans are known as "baksoo mudangs," while the female shamans are called "mudangs." They are given their positions either through hereditary descent or by displaying natural shamanistic abilities. Cultures in Siberia, Mongolia, Malaysia, and the Philippines also have shamanistic traditions, where shamans are held in high regard.

India has several practices very similar to shamanism, although they use names like the "Nechung Oracle," which serves the same function as a shaman. Even the Dalai Lama consults the oracle for spiritual advice, and the Nechung Oracle is the official state oracle of the Tibetan government. In Nepal, shamans are known as "Jhakri," and the Sunuwar, Tamang, Limbu, Kami, Sherpa, Rai, Gurung, Lepcha, and Magar people all have Jhakri within their communities. The Jhakri are also influenced by the traditions of Tibetan Buddhism, Hinduism, Mun, and Bön.

The Americas

In North American indigenous cultures like the Native Americans and First Nations, traditional roles exist, such as mystics, lore-keepers, healers, medicine people, and singers that greatly resemble shamans. However, the actual term "shaman" has never been used to describe these religious figures, instead giving them unique terms in their own languages. Not all indigenous cultures have a religious figure who communicates with the spiritual realm, connecting the living members of the community to the spirits. Those with a variety of traditions and beliefs are associated with the role, but the commonalities between them are very similar to the duties of a traditional shaman.

Ancient Mesoamerican cultures, including the Mayas and Aztecs, had members of the priesthood who performed the traditional shamanistic role. The Mayas had a class of priests who were specifically tasked as shamans, maintaining a complex network that crossed the entire empire. They used divination, healing rituals, dream interpretation, astrology, and trances to communicate with spirits within the spiritual realm. The Aztecs had priests who performed a similar function, and one of the major gods of their pantheon was Tezcatlipoca, which meant "smoking mirror," who was a Pan-Mesoamerican shaman god with omnipotence and universal power.

South American cultures such as the Urarina of the Peruvian Amazon, the Santo Daime, and União do Vegetal religions, the Mapuche people of Chile, the Aymara people, and the indigenous people of Tierra del Fuego all have variations of shamanistic traditions. The Urarina people, as well as the Santo Daime and União do Vegetal religions, use the entheogen called ayahuasca during shamanistic rituals as a primary aspect of their society, connecting to the spiritual realm to gain guidance from divine spirits. Their shamans are highly regarded members of society, aiding the people in finding their place in the world and fulfilling their destinies. The Urarina call their shamans "ayahuasqueros," and their ayahuasca brews have been said to be a cure-all for maladies from addiction to depression and even cancer.

There are tribes in the Amazon rainforest whose shamans also serve to manage the scarcity of ecological resources. As deforestation plagues the rainforest, they attempt to mitigate the damage by overseeing replanting efforts. There is a tribe known as the Waiwai who have members of the community called the "yaskomo." They are essentially shamans, performing "soul flights" for healing, consulting cosmological beings for advice, and sending their souls down into the depths of the river to gain the aid of divine beings dwelling there. A yaskomo is able to make contact with the earth, the sky, and the water.

The Mapuche have "machis," women who perform ceremonial rituals to ward off evil spirits, cure diseases, and control the weather and harvest yields. The Aymara have a "Yatiri" who heals both the body and the soul and serves the community through performing rituals for Pachamama. One aspect of their healing abilities comes through certain shamanistic practices that use plant alkaloids consumed during therapeutic sessions. They believe that balancing the mind and soul makes it easier to mend the body.

In Tierra del Fuego, the indigenous people known as the Fuegians had a hunter-gatherer culture. Still, their religious practices were not homogenized across all the tribes. The Selk'nam and Yámana people were two Fuegian tribes that had shamanistic roles within their cultures. They believed their shamans had supernatural abilities, could control the weather, and communicate with their gods and other divine beings. The shamans also performed sacred rituals to help their hunters find and kill game animals for food and other rituals to aid with the foraging of resources and supplies.

Modern Latin American and some Spanish-based communities in the United States have a figure known as a "curandero," who specializes in both Western and traditional medicine, using techniques from both to help treat the physical, mental, emotional, and spiritual illnesses that can afflict their people. The Catholic Church also influences their form of shamanism. The curanderos will use traditional shamanistic methods combined with Catholic rituals or rites, including prayers, holy water, and religious imagery, to assist in their duties.

Europe

Across Eastern, Western, and Southern Europe, shamanism has a long tradition dating back to the ancient pre-Christian cultures in the region. In Italy, there was an agrarian cult known as the Benandanti, which had shamans that induced trances where they combated witches in a spiritual battle to save their people's crops. Many Germanic peoples had shamans tied closely with their warriors and magical beliefs. A type of warrior known as "berserkers" used trance-inducing rituals to send them into a frenzied state where they could fight without feeling pain. These practices were administered or overseen by a tribe's shaman leaders.

Shamanism in Northern Europe

In Northern Europe, the Nordic people were heavily influenced by the beliefs and practices of the pre-Christian Germanic cultures. They had a role called a Völva that acted as a shaman, offering guidance and spiritual advice to the members of their culture. The Welsh had soothsayers and prophets called the "awenyddion," who gave ominous prophecies in a deep trance in response to those seeking them for divine guidance. When an awenyddion was sought out for their expertise, it was customary to bring a token or gift to serve as an offering that could be used to help the awenyddion draw a stronger connection to the divine powers while in their trance.

Shamanism has long been associated with Gaelic traditions in Ireland and Scotland. Many tales and historical accounts include shamanistic aspects within Celtic cultures. Shamans are associated with heroes and leaders, usually taking an advisory role and utilizing their connection to the spiritual realm to gain knowledge of secrets and future events. This is particularly true with the stories involving King Arthur, where Merlin exhibits many traits of a shaman. The figures that Merlin is believed to be based on, Myrddin and Ambrosius, can similarly be viewed as shamanistic due to their prophetic abilities and connection to the spiritual realm. There is a rich history of shamanism in Celtic society, which has continued to the present day.

Chapter 2: What Is a Celtic Shaman?

Celtic shamanism has its roots in the British Isles, where it is believed to have been practiced by ancient indigenous cultures and early settlers. In Ireland, the Gaelic people native to the island had societal roles that were very clearly shamanistic. There was also a strong shamanistic component to the West Germanic tribes known as the Angles, Saxons, Frisians, and Jutes, who arrived in southern England following the withdrawal of the Roman invaders, while some of the Celtic Britons who already dwelt in the region and had been partially Romanized similarly upheld certain customs of shamanism. In Scotland, the native Picts and Gaels, as well as the Germanic-speaking Angles who came from Northumbria, maintained shamanistic traditions as well.

Stonehenge, a prehistoric monument located in Wiltshire, England.
https://unsplash.com/photos/Hl8LPagOrKs

Celtic Shamanism in Ireland

The Gaels who lived in Ireland before the arrival of the Vikings displayed many beliefs and customs associated with shamanism. The mythological tales formulated by the culture included a spiritual realm known as the "Otherworld," where their deities and the souls of the dead resided. The Otherworld figures appear in many myths and legends that developed during the earliest eras of Ireland. When the Vikings arrived in the 9th century, causing the people to become the Norse-Gaels, the similarities in traditional religious beliefs between the Gaelic and Norse cultures caused their mythology and customs to mesh fairly well.

Around the 12th century, Anglo-Norman invaders conquered portions of the country, while the later 16th and 17th-century colonization by England brought many English and people from the Scottish Lowlands to the northern regions. These new cultures' influence caused shamanism's evolution into a more homogenized form, and modern Celtic shamanism traces its ancestry back through the ages to all these different lineages. Because Ireland still maintains a strong Celtic character, many pockets of communities have brought Celtic shamanism into the 21st century.

Celtic Shamanism in England and Wales

The traditions of shamanism in England and Wales primarily stemmed from the Angles and Saxons, particularly after they transformed into the Anglo-Saxons. The Frisians and Jutes possessed some aspects of shamanism within their cultures. As they became absorbed by the Anglo-Saxon people following the incursion of the Romans into the British Isles, it developed a distinctly Celtic flavor. Once Christianity began to spread throughout Europe and arrived in England and Wales, the tug-of-war between the pagan and Christian religions eventually ended in favor of the latter.

Celtic Shamanism in Scotland

The Picts and Gaels who dwelt in ancient Scotland were both Celtic; therefore, they had shamanistic traditions like their brethren in Ireland. During the Roman conquest of the British Isles, the Romans never managed to gain much territory in Scotland, and the constant warfare between the natives and the invaders eventually resulted in the construction of Hadrian's Wall, built by the Roman emperor Hadrian, and the Antonine Wall erected by Hadrian's successor, Antoninus Pius.

By the 5th century, the Romans had been mostly driven out of the British Isles, and the Saxons moved into Scotland.

Around the 6th century, Scotland was divided between the Picts, the Anglo-Saxons, and the Gaelic settlers from Ireland. Vikings later supplanted these cultures in the Northern Isles of Orkney and Shetland, and there was some Norse influence on the mainland afterward. This mix of Celtic, Anglo-Saxon, and Pictish cultures had Christian and pagan characteristics, while shamanism in the region took on aspects of both religions. The practitioners of shamanism in Scotland during the Middle Ages were sometimes regarded with suspicion. Still, their abilities to commune with the spiritual realm and their knowledge of herbalism and healing made them indispensable to their communities.

The Celts

Determining how to define who the Celts are can be tricky. Historically, there has been debate over whether to consider them an ethnicity, language, or culture. Currently, most modern scholars define Celts as "speakers of the Celtic languages" rather than any ethnocultural group. The primary historical Celtic peoples include the Britons, the Boii, the Celtiberians, the Gaels, the Gauls, the Gallaeci, the Galatians, and the Lepontii, as well as their offshoots. The six living Celtic languages are Breton, Irish, Scottish Gaelic, Welsh, Cornish, and Manx. The first four are considered continuous living languages, as they have been spoken by an unbroken line of cultures, while the latter two are revived languages, having once fallen out of use, but resurrected and reconstructed.

Extinct Dialects of the Celtic Language

There have been sixteen dialects of the Celtic language spoken throughout history, but ten of them have gone extinct. Most of the dead dialects were only spoken by people not native to the British Isles and had primarily developed in Continental Europe. The Celtic languages that have gone extinct include Celtiberian, Gallic, Noric, Galwegian Gaelic, Cumbric, Cisalpine Gaulish, Transalpine Gaulish, Pictish, Galatian, and Lepontic. Due to these languages evolving from foreign influences and the later Roman conquest of both Continental Europe and parts of the British Isles, they eventually disappeared and became considered extinct.

Shamans of the Celtic People

The shamans found among the ancient Celtic people had a certain mystical aura about them. There is little doubt that their contemporaries felt that they appeared peculiar to an extent. The use of entheogens, inducing a trance-like state in which they could commune with the spiritual realm, and their abilities to speak to both living and dead spirits set them apart from the rest of their society. Shamans were both loved and feared since they could seemingly discern secrets they shouldn't have been able to uncover without ever speaking to another living being. This gave them a position of prominence in their culture, but they remained separate from everyone else.

The Roles of Shamans

Most shamans of the Celtic people in the British Isles were considered revered elders and advisors, and in some cases, even leaders of their people. They possessed a mastery over spiritual and medicinal matters, making them akin to doctors and priests. Whenever a member of their tribe or village got sick or injured, the afflicted individuals would be sent to see their local shaman. Through a variety of means, the shaman would practice their craft to render aid and medical assistance to the ailing party. This included the application of medicinal herbs and poultices, as well as certain consumable concoctions to help ease the effects of certain illnesses and injuries.

If members of the community were in need of advice, they would often consult their shaman, who sought answers from the spirits. They were also responsible for determining which spirits were benevolent and which were malevolent, seeking only to cause chaos among the people. Trickster spirits were especially dangerous since they sometimes posed as benevolent ones, offering seemingly-innocuous advice that was actually meant to harm the individual in question. A good shaman could figure out when a spirit was trying to deceive them, warding them off through rituals and prayers.

Spirituality in Shamanism

Spirituality within shamanism refers to the search for meaning and a purpose in life in relation to the sanctity of the world. Part of a shaman's mandate is to assist the people of their community in finding their sacred meaning or purpose. This often resulted in the shaman serving as a guide as an individual undertook a vision quest, overseeing the person's spiritual journey as they confronted their inner mind and soul. Some of this guidance would come through interpreting the imagery and symbolism that a person saw while on their vision quest. It wasn't up to a shaman to tell the individual what their purpose might be, hey would merely help lead each person to the conclusions made on their own.

Magic in Shamanism

As it relates to shamanism, magic is very closely linked to the kind practiced by Wicca and Druidry. The purpose of their magic is to affect the living world through rituals, spells, prayers, and divination. It is a manipulation of the energy that dwells within all living things and the power of the soul. This can also be called an "aura," which is the potential energy emitted by humans, animals, flora, and the elements. Learning how to harness this potential energy and tap into it to use magic is one of the main goals of all shamans.

However, do not mistake shamanistic magic for the type of magic typically seen in works of fiction. They do not cast thunderbolts or throw fireballs around, and there is certainly no sparkling energy spewing out of magic wands. Real magic is subtler, working invisibly to cause a change in the potential energy that exists all around us. When using magic, it can be difficult for an external observer to actually identify what is occurring with it. Even the person affected by magic may not realize what has been done, chalking up their experiences to pure luck.

Shamanism and the Celtic Pagans

Unlike other religious practices, shamanism does not necessarily include a single supreme being or a pantheon of gods. Instead, the spirits of the dead, animals, and personifications of abstract concepts are the primary "higher powers" with which they commune. It can be seen as more of a supplemental religion typically practiced alongside more traditional religions, such as paganism or monotheistic deism. Shamans' main responsibility was to the people, whereas priests or Druids were beholden to the gods.

The Celtic paganism that arose in the British Isles before the Christianization of the area included a pantheon with various gods. The specific brand of shamanism practiced by the Celtic culture was influenced by this, such as a larger role played by the elements and nature, which can sometimes cause confusion between shamans and

Druids. However, while Druids focused on nature itself, shamans were chiefly concerned with the spirits that exist as an extension of nature.

Chapter 3: Who Are the Druids?

Druids were among the highest-ranking members of ancient Celtic society. They were not merely religious leaders. They also served as keepers of lore, healers, adjudicators, legal authorities, and political advisors. There were many similarities between Druids and shamans in Celtic culture, but they had enough differences that the roles were not interchangeable. It was not uncommon for a community to have both Druids and shamans serving them.

Druids were among the highest-ranking members of ancient Celtic society.
Simon King, CC BY-SA 4.0 <https://creativecommons.org/licenses/by-sa/4.0>, via Wikimedia Commons: https://commons.wikimedia.org/wiki/File:Druids_on_Primrose_Hill_Autumn_Equinox.jpg

History of the Druids

The first extensive references to the existence of Druids came from the Bellum Gallicum by Julius Caesar in 58-49 BCE. In it, he described the various roles of Druids living in Gaul, inhabited by both the Celtic and Aquitani tribes. Caesar wrote about their religious practices and societal hierarchy, including how most Druids remained in power for the duration of their lifetime. Interestingly, while a Druid leader's successor sometimes came to power through violence, more often than not, a new one was chosen through popular vote. While Caesar's scholarship focused on Druids in Continental Europe, it is likely to be very close to how Druidry worked in the British Isles.

In ancient Wales, Druids were some of the most important members of Celtic society. Although there are no written records concerning their earliest appearances, oral traditions usually date their presence in Wales to at least the 4th century BCE, but they may have been around much earlier. They were revered by the people they led, as they were viewed as the definitive link between humanity, nature, and the gods. Stonehenge, a prehistoric monument in Wiltshire, England, is believed to have been built sometime during the 30th or 29th century BCE. It is theorized to have been raised by the Druids as a sacred ceremonial site where they practiced important religious gatherings and rituals.

With the Roman conquest of the British Isles between 43-87 AD and the advent of Christianity, the Druids were pushed further and further toward the fringes of society. Christian priests and other church leaders were given prominence, diminishing the influence that Druids were able to exert. While Druidry survived in some form until the Middle Ages, it became effectively extinct not long after, being consigned to a few isolated pockets in England, Scotland, and Ireland, where practitioners struggled to preserve their religion amid an ever-increasing irrelevance. Some aspects of Christianity in the British Isles adopted Druid themes and symbols, syncretizing parts of Druidry with their own sacred figures and practices.

It wasn't until the 18th century that a renewed interest in Druidry resulted in its revival as a neopagan religion. One of the first neopagan Druidic organizations was founded in 1781 by Henry Hurle called the Ancient Order of Druids (AOD). The Druid Order is another major religious group that was founded by a man named George Watson

MacGregor Reid in 1909. These religions sought to recreate as closely as possible their historical counterparts. However, one part of ancient Druidry not retained was the ritualistic sacrifices that many asserted they practiced, including sacrificing both sacred animals and human beings. This was due to the growing awareness of human and animal rights that started to take hold in the British Isles and society at large. In other areas, the Romanticism movement also tended to avoid the darker parts of the culture in favor of an overly generous depiction of the past. This is where the idea of the "noble savage" was first developed.

Roles of Druids

Druids were leaders and high-ranking members of their communities, being at the top of the three tiers with prominent warriors and serfs below them. However, this was not their only role in Celtic society. They often served a wide range of functions, making them indispensable to their people. In many instances, a Druidic leader was one of the few literate people in their community, placing the responsibility on them to carry out tasks that others were not equipped to handle. Their education and scholarship allowed them to gain insight into subjects that might otherwise elude their fellow tribespeople. This resulted in the Druid leaders bearing the burden of compiling their knowledge and wisdom into a form that could be passed down to future generations.

As keepers of lore, Druids were the authority on Celtic deities and history. They didn't maintain many written records but passed the lore on through oral traditions. Druids also used their depth of knowledge to serve their people by seeing to their medical needs. Being educated, they had experience with herbs and medical techniques to aid any sick or injured community members. While this aspect of Druidry has some overlap with shamanism, shamans typically focused on healing through spiritual means, while Druids sought to use their knowledge about nature to treat the physical symptoms.

Druids were often the final word on matters of law and justice. They were the arbiters of conflict and adjudicators who handed down a final judgment when people were accused of criminal acts. In this role, Druids had quite a bit of leeway regarding how they chose to punish those accused of breaking the law, with execution or exile being the harshest penalties one could incur. However, in most cases, a Druid would need to step in to render judgment due to conflicts over land, property, and interpersonal issues. Since there was no codified set of legal regulations for Druids, how they chose to handle each matter was entirely up to them.

While Druids usually held a leadership position within their community, they were not always the ultimate authority. In the instances where a secular leader held a higher station of power than them, they would serve as a political advisor, much the same as shamans. This became more common as society shifted from a religious focus to putting more emphasis on martial prowess. A warrior chieftain would have total control over their clan or tribe but would still consult with their Druids before making any politically significant decisions, especially regarding their interactions with rival groups.

Beliefs of Druids

Druidry has a core set of beliefs that remained consistent from its earliest days to the present time. It is these beliefs that both set it apart from and make it compatible with shamanism. The similarities between the two are significant enough that they are often confused. Still, it's a mistake to use the terms "Druid" and "shaman" interchangeably. Highlighting the common features as well as the differences can help to exemplify their relationship with each other.

Lack of Dogma

Somewhat paradoxically, one of Druidry's core beliefs is that they don't have a rigid belief system. As a religion, there is a stronger emphasis on personal experience than on pre-established tenets. Unlike Christianity, there are no strict commandments concerning how a practitioner behaves or the actions they can and cannot take. This lack of dogma makes Druidry much more of a loose affiliation of ideas and concepts than a belief system with firm boundaries.

Nature Worship

Nature is a major facet of Druidry, as many of their practices stem from believing in nature as a divine source. While some Druids are animists like shamans, they view nature's power as a construct in and of itself rather than possessing energy that manifests in the spiritual realm. There is a preoccupation with maintaining balance within nature, ensuring that a healthy life cycle can be perpetuated endlessly. This can be seen in how Druids will regard certain parts of nature as personifications of divine beings, such as worshiping certain deities, such as the god Dagda and goddess Daron through oak trees.

The Afterlife

The concept of an afterlife doesn't exist in Druidry in the same way in other religions, such as the Christian belief in Heaven, Hell, Purgatory, and Limbo. Instead, they maintain that those who die can return through reincarnation. The Druidic perspective is that those whose spiritual power is potent enough will return to the living world as a new being, either human, animal, or an important part of nature. They also believe that some people will transition from the world of the living to a peaceful, all-encompassing afterlife known as the Otherworld.

The Otherworld

The Otherworld in Druidry is similar to the shamanistic version with the same name. After a person has fulfilled their ultimate purpose in life, they are rewarded by passing on to the Otherworld, where they get the chance to dwell among mythological beings and deities. Suppose someone should decide that they would prefer to return to the living world. In that case, they may be given the opportunity to be reincarnated. However, the specific form that their new physical body takes is often left up to the whims of the higher powers.

Interconnectivity

Like shamanism, Druids have a belief in the interconnectivity of all life. However, where they differ is in the actual way this interconnection works. Shamans focus on the relationship between the physical world and the spiritual realm. In contrast, Druids view interconnectivity as the web of life between humans, animals, and the rest of nature. Plants, flowers, and trees provide oxygen, fruits, vegetables, and other resources, with smaller animals feeding on nuts and plants and larger animals consuming the smaller ones. Humans eat animals, grains, fruits, and vegetables while utilizing other natural resources, planting new seeds, or protecting crops while maintaining natural harmony.

Magic

Magic is a key component of Druidry, even more so than in other contemporary religions. Most of the magic that makes up the Druidic belief system is rooted in nature, with the goal being a balance between all living things. They use rituals, spells, prayers, relics, and divination to help them employ magic for the benefit of their people. To Druids, magic is another natural part of the world, and using it is no different than starting a fire to cook and keep warm or collecting water for washing and drinking. They believe that nature is filled with magical energy that can be harnessed and redirected to aid in their endeavors.

Modern Druids

Modern Druids come from a neopagan tradition that has painstakingly recreated the ancient Druidic religion from all available sources, making it as authentic as possible. Most modern Druids are members of this religious movement, and while there are official organizations like the Druid Order and the AOD, not every Druid is required to be part of them. Some operate independently, looking to the forebears' example to guide their actions as leaders, healers, and protectors of nature.

The Ancient Order of Druids

The AOD is the oldest continuous Druidic order in the modern world. In a nod to the position within the society of their ancient ancestors, their motto is "Justice, Philanthropy, and Brotherly Love." They are active in the United Kingdom and France, operating branches across both counties. The AOD is run by the Imperial Grand Arch-Druid, and the person on whom that title is conferred is normally chosen through a vote by their regular members. The order attempts to assimilate their beliefs and actions into the modern world, volunteering within their communities and assisting with charitable endeavors. There is a strong emphasis on protecting nature, especially as environmental issues are rapidly becoming a hot topic throughout the Western world.

The Druid Order

The Druid Order propagates a philosophy of personal experience over academic learning, believing that any information gained from books or the classroom is not as useful as the wisdom acquired through actions in the real world. They also strongly focus on meditation as an overarching activity for all members. When the order holds meetings, they will discuss topics that range from philosophy, mythology, astrology, poetry, and history to debates on contemporary politics and religion. The highest authority within the Druid Order is a position known as the Chief Druid, who generally serves for whatever length of time they desire and normally chooses their successor personally.

Practices of Modern Druids

Because modern Druidry is both a revival and an extension of ancient Druidry, they share many of the same beliefs and practices. Other than ritual sacrifices, they maintain the traditions popular throughout the British Isles in the pre-Roman and pre-Christian eras. Keeping in mind that the world has changed quite a bit since that time, neopagan practitioners of Druidry have learned how to integrate their belief system into modern society, such as utilizing communication tools like the internet to connect with one another over long distances and across regional borders.

As the development of human civilization continues to extend into the untouched pockets of nature that have remained undisturbed, modern Druids serve as advocates for the environment. They seek to remind people of the beauty and power of the natural world and the benefits of keeping existing ecosystems intact. With many groups of animals becoming endangered and on their way to extinction, it is more important than ever for the Druidic philosophy to have a voice within modern cultures. If we're not careful enough to preserve nature, it could have dire consequences for future generations.

Druids vs. Shaman

For a quick overview of Druids versus shamans, you can refer to this chart below:

Druidry	Shamanism
Roles: Community leader; healer; political advisor; adjudicator; legal authority; lore keeper	Roles: Spiritual, political, and personal advisor; healer; seer; cultural leader
Afterlife: Reincarnation; the Otherworld	Afterlife: The spiritual realm (lower, middle, upper levels); the Otherworld
Interconnectivity: Humans, animals, and nature	Interconnectivity: The physical world and spiritual realm

Focus: Nature	Focus: Spirits
Magic: Spells; rituals; sacrifices; divination; prayers	Magic: Visions; vision quests; trances; rituals; prayers; divination; spells

Chapter 4: Celtic Deities and Symbols

Part of Celtic paganism is its unique mythology and symbols. As with many religions, these are important to the larger culture, providing tales of historically-significant figures intermingled with mythical heroes and gods and giving meaning through imagery and iconography. Celtic paganism doesn't have a strict "pantheon" like other religions, such as the Greek and Roman pagans or Norse and Egyptian mythology. Instead, it is more of a loose affiliation of deities that are culturally important and worshiped on an individual basis.

Part of Celtic paganism is its unique mythology and symbols.
Art Gongs, CC BY-SA 4.0 <https://creativecommons.org/licenses/by-sa/4.0>, via Wikimedia Commons: https://commons.wikimedia.org/wiki/File:Celtic_Tree_Of_Life_Art_Gong.jpg

Celtic Deities

There is a wide variety of Celtic deities due to the disparity between those worshiped regionally and those with a universal place within the religion. Many of these deities fall into categories based on specific characteristics, sharing these features with different deities that change from one locale to another. In Ireland, the primary gods are known as the Tuatha Dé Danann, who fought both the Fir Bolg and the Fomorians for dominion of the Otherworld. Welsh mythology sets its deities in the real world, but gods and supernatural beings exist alongside Arthurian heroes and villains. Here is a list of the different categories for the Celtic deities, as well as the most prominent ones within them:

Chief Gods

The chief gods are those who are considered either great leaders or important mythological figures. They include:

Lugh

A major warrior king and chief god who is usually depicted as part of the Tuatha Dé Danann. Lugh appears primarily in Irish mythology, although variants have shown up in other regions. The main features of Lugh include his weapon, known as the Spear of Assal, which was said to be impossible to overcome, and his mighty horse, Aenbharr, that could carry him at great speeds across both land and water. Lugh is involved in many tales within the Irish mythological cycle, and he lends his name to the pagan harvest festival of Lughnasadh.

Taranis

A god of thunder who is sometimes equated with Zeus or Jupiter and has been worshiped in Ireland, Britain, Hispania, and Gaul. Taranis is usually shown wielding a lightning bolt in one hand and a solar wheel in the other. Due to his position as a thunder god, he is considered a chief god in many regions that practiced Celtic paganism. However, his exact status is not always the same. In some locales, Taranis is above all other gods, while in other places, he is seen as one or two tiers below the local chief god.

Toutatis

Considered a protector of tribes, taking up his war hammer to smite the foes of those he is charged with safeguarding. Many Celtic tales place him alongside Lugh and Taranis as a trio of chief gods, and Toutatis has been equated to both Hermes/Mercury and Ares/Mars. As a skilled and dangerous warrior, he is typically said to be invincible in battle, and at other times, he is shown as a healer. Ancient Roman sources claimed that the Celtic pagans would make human sacrifices to Toutatis by casting people headfirst into a vat of an unknown liquid.

Esus

A god of the ancient Celtic Britons and Celtic pagans in Gaul, he was typically depicted as a large, axe-wielding warrior. One of the most famous images of Esus shows him hewing trees with his massive axe. Esus' name means passion, energy, and well-being, so he can be interpreted as a virile figure of battle and protection. In some traditions, he will aid those who invoke his name through a magical charm. Like Toutatis, Esus is associated with human sacrifice, and people were sacrificed to him during a ritual that included tying the victim to a tree and flogging them to death.

Mother Goddesses

The mother goddesses in Celtic paganism are known as "matronae," meaning "matrons." These goddesses tend to be closely identified with nature and the earth. The regional variants of the matronae include:

Modron, Rhiannon, and Dôn

These three are Welsh deities who represent different aspects of the mother goddess. Modron can be translated to "great mother," Rhiannon means "great queen," while Dôn is the mother of three important mythological figures who are known collectively as the "Children of Dôn." Modron is noted as the mother of Mabon ap Modron, who was said to be part of King Arthur's warband in the older Welsh version of Arthurian mythology. Some scholars have equated Modron with the later character of Morgan le Fay; thus, her son is seen as the precursor to Sir Mordred.

Rhiannon is a strong motherly figure who originated in the Otherworld and rules over a realm alongside her chosen consort, Pwyll Pen Annwn. She is often described as a giantess who is as strong as a horse, able to carry a dozen men upon her back. Some stories depict her as riding slowly across the Otherworld, always in view yet always out of reach. Because of her connection to horses, Rhiannon is sometimes compared to the Gaulish goddess Epona, who is usually shown in the form of a mare.

Dôn represents the power of motherhood through birthing and raising a trio of heroic figures. Her older son Gwydion fab Dôn is a trickster hero and magician. Her younger son Gilfaethwy is constantly living in his brother's shadow, and his deeds can be viewed as less heroic, although he suffers a magical form of punishment that is reminiscent of the twelve labors of Hercules. Her daughter Arianrhod is cursed by a mythical Welsh king and must outsmart him in order to break the three curses and gain her freedom.

Boand, Ernmas, Danu, and Macha

These are Irish deities who represent the mother goddess category in a similar manner to their Welsh counterparts. Boand is well known for giving birth to the god Aengus by having an affair with Dagda while her husband Elcmar is sent away on an errand. When he returns, Dagda hides Boand's pregnancy by causing the sun to stand still, preventing Elcmar from noticing the passage of time. Nine months later, Aengus is born, and Dagda restarts the sun. This has been proposed to be an ancient mythological origin for the dark, cold winter months.

Ernmas is notable for giving birth to three important trinities of children that feature heavily in the Irish variation of Celtic mythology. The eldest trio consists of Ériu, Fódla, and Banba, a trinity of war goddesses. The middle trio consists of the goddesses known as the Morrígan, named Anann, Badb, and Macha. The youngest trio consists of three sons: Coscar, Glonn, and Gnim. Unfortunately, despite the fame of her children, Ernmas was killed early on during the First Battle of Mag Tuired, when the Tuatha Dé Danann prevailed over the Fir Bolg.

Danu is considered the mother goddess of the Tuatha Dé Danann, an ancestor of the many deities in Irish mythology. Macha is an earth and sovereignty goddess heavily associated with the Irish province of Ulster. She is also a daughter of Ernmas and a member of the Morrígan, representing a warrior's glorious death in battle. She and her sisters are also seen as omens of doom and are related to the figure of the banshee in later Irish folklore.

Healing Deities

The healing deities in Celtic paganism come from numerous sources. They are often associated with herbalism, thermal springs, healing wells, and light. The healing deities include:

Brighid and Airmed

Brighid and Airmed are Irish goddesses known for their healing powers. Brighid is a member of the Tuatha Dé Danann, and she is a patron of not just healing but also wisdom, poetry, blacksmithing, protection, and domesticated animals. She is also related to the Celtic Briton goddess Brigantia, representing victory in war. Airmed participated in the Second Battle of Mag Tuired, healing anyone injured on the battlefield. After her father killed her brother, she wept at his grave for so long that her tears watered the earth, giving rise to all the healing herbs throughout the world.

Dian Cécht

A god of healing who was one of the Tuatha Dé Danann, fighting in the battles against both the Fir Bolgs and the Fomorians. Dian Cécht would heal the injured by submerging them in a healing well. When Nuada, the first king of the Tuatha Dé Danann, lost his arm during one of the wars against the Fomorians, Dian Cécht made him a new one out of silver, but it was able to function like a normal arm. However, when Dian Cécht's son, Miach, was able to fashion a flesh and blood arm to replace the silver one, Dian Cécht killed him out of jealousy. The tears of his daughter, Airmed, gave rise to all the healing herbs in the world, but after she collected them in one place, Dian Cécht again became jealous, scattering them across the four winds and preventing anyone from having complete knowledge of every healing herb in existence.

Belenus, Borvo, and Grannus

They are Celtic gods of healing who were worshiped in parts of Britain conquered by the Romans. Belenus is similar to the god Apollo and is closely associated with horses and chariots. Occasionally, he has been depicted as riding a horse-drawn chariot across the sky, carrying the sun with him like Apollo. Borvo is believed to offer healing through thermal springs, and it's said that he has infused the water with a special salve known only to him. Grannus is also related to thermal springs and mineral water, but it is more the soothing aspect of heat that is claimed to be his forte.

Water Deities

As one of the four elements, water is an incredibly important part of Celtic life. All living things require water to survive, and using it for cleansing purposes has given it an association with purity and virginity. Water gods and goddesses in Celtic paganism include:

Manannán, Lir, and Nodens

These three gods are water deities, but each one represents slightly different aspects of this element. Manannán is a great warrior and king who lived in the Otherworld, where he is a god of the sea. He has a boat called the Sguaba Tuinne, or Wave-Sweeper, that can propel itself across the water. Manannán also possesses the power to use mist from the ocean to make himself and his surroundings completely invisible to human eyes. Lir is the father of Manannán and the god of the oceans. He is a personification of the fury of the sea, exhibited by large waves crashing against the shore or tossing sailing vessels to and fro as if they were mere toys. Nodens is part healer and part warrior and is associated with the sea and hunting dogs.

Sulis, Damona, and Bormana

These goddesses are both water deities and healing deities, as they represent water's healing and purification properties. Sulis is a Celtic goddess worshiped in Britain, and she is a patron of the thermal spring near the city of Bath that is believed to encourage recovery and rejuvenation. While she is a life-giving and nourishing deity, her name is also invoked in several curses meant to strike down the foes of her venerators. Damona and Bormana both inhabit similar roles, being female counterparts to the god Borvo. They are associated with water and thermal springs like Borvo, with Damona linked to the hot spring at Bourbonne-les-Bains, and Bormana to the one in Saint-Vulbas.

Antlered Deities

The antlered deities in Celtic paganism typically represent hunters, the wilderness, and wild animals. Due to their association with a stag, the antlered deities are considered male, and part of their power comes from their masculinity. The antlered deities include:

Cernunnos

He is an Irish god who is usually shown sitting cross-legged and surrounded by bulls, stags, rams, horned serpents, and dogs. Cernunnos is a figure of great power and can be seen as a counterpart to the mother goddesses. As with other antlered gods, he symbolizes male potency and the untamed wilderness. Some stories depict Cernunnos as a heroic figure, aiding demigods such as Fráech when he attempts to rescue his wife and son from evil beings who kidnapped them during a cattle raid.

Brân the Blessed

A Welsh god, sometimes depicted as a horned giant, is a mythical high king. Brân is known to be a skilled hunter, often riding his massive steed both into battle and on the trail of dangerous prey. His name is translated as "crow" or "raven." As an interesting aside, author George R. R. Martin has used the name "Bran" for a character in his book series "A Song of Ice and Fire," later adapted into the television series "Game of Thrones." In the narrative, Bran is closely associated with a being known as the Three-Eyed Crow or Bloodraven.

Other Deities

Many other deities are connected to Celtic paganism. The concepts they represent vary wildly, including hammers, eloquence, horses, divine bulls, and the sun. The deities belonging to these different categories include:

Sun Goddesses: Áine and Olwen

Áine and Olwen are both considered sun goddesses, although scholars have sometimes questioned their status as solar deities. In Irish mythology, Áine is associated with the midsummer sun, possessing the qualities of sovereignty and wealth. Because she represents the summer, she is occasionally depicted as a red mare with a fiery mane and hooves. Olwen is said to be as beautiful as the burning sun, wearing a red dress engulfed in flames, having bright yellow hair that looks like fire, and adorned with many golden rings.

God of Hammers: Sucellos

A Celtic god who is always shown holding an enormous hammer or mallet. Despite this, he is typically worshiped as a god of agriculture, wine, and beer. The reason he is always carrying a hammer or mallet is unknown, but several tales call him a "good striker," implying that he can use his weapon in battle when necessary. In addition, Sucellos protects the fields and forests and serves as a guardian of boundaries. He has also been equated with Silvanus, the Roman god of the forests. Both are known to have protected flocks of sheep from hungry wolves, skinning and wearing the pelts of those they have slain.

Gods of Eloquence and Strength: Ogmios and Oghma

Ogmios is a Celtic god of eloquence and strength, using his persuasive abilities to bind men to his causes. However, he is also noted for his superhuman strength and able to perform incredible feats of physical prowess. He can be seen as an analog to both Heracles and Odysseus from Greek mythology. Oghma is a similar god from Irish mythology, serving as the champion of Nuada, king of the Tuatha Dé Danann. He is credited as the creator of Ogham, the Celtic tree alphabet.

Horse Deities: Epona and Atepomarus

Epona is a horse goddess in Celtic mythology, originally worshiped by the people of Gaul and later migrating to the British Isles. She is a goddess of fertility and a protector of horses, ponies, mules, and donkeys. In some traditions, she serves as a psychopomp, leading her steeds as they carry souls into the afterlife. Atepomarus, also associated with horses, is also a healer. His name can translate to "great horseman," and when venerated by the Celts, they would leave small horse figurines around his shrines.

The Divine Bull: Tarvos Trigaranus

He is a Celtic god who takes on the form of a large bull and is associated with Esus. In artwork depicting both Tarvos Trigaranus and Esus, the former usually looms over the latter but is somewhat hidden behind or within a tree that Esus is chopping down. As the Divine Bull, Tarvos Trigaranus represents power, potency, stamina, hard work, determination, confidence, and wealth. The ancient Celtic pagans would sometimes sacrifice a bull during religious ceremonies, as an offering of such magnitude was often taken as a sign of great respect.

Celtic Symbols

Many symbols, images, and iconography are considered sacred to the Celtic people. Each of these represents aspects of Celtic society that are deemed important or relevant to their daily lives. Some symbols possess religious connotations, while others are more defined by cultural traits. The following list includes the Celtic symbols that are most often associated with their people:

The Celtic Cross: ⊕

The Celtic Cross is a variation on the Latin cross, appearing like a lowercase "t" with a circle around the intersection of the two limbs. This is sometimes interpreted as a halo. It originated in Ireland during the Middle Ages, around the time when Christianity began to spread across the British Isles, pushing the Celtic pagans to the fringes of society. To avoid being completely usurped, the Celtic people adopted some of the imagery from Christianity, incorporating it into their own iconography. There are different interpretations of what the Celtic Cross signifies. Some believe the four limbs represent the four Cardinal directions (north, south, east, and west). In contrast, others claim it symbolizes the four seasons (spring, summer, autumn, and winter) or the four stages of the day (morning, midday, evening, and midnight).

The Celtic Tree of Life:

The Celtic Tree of Life is called "Crann Bethadh" in Irish. It is usually depicted as a large tree with interwoven roots and branches. It is a symbol often associated with Druids. The Tree of Life represents harmony and balance, as its branches hold up the sky and its roots anchor the earth. This symbol is often created symmetrically so that it appears the same upside down and right side up. Since many Celtic cultures believed that spirits were dwelling within the trees, sometimes even the spirits of their ancestors, the Tree of Life provided a link between this world and the next.

The Triquetra:

The Triquetra is also known as the Celtic Triangle or the Trinity Knot. It has a continuous three-pointed symbol reminiscent of the shape of a leaf interwoven with a circle. The Triquetra represents unity, family, and eternal love, displaying the interlocking shapes as members of a family unit. Scholars believe it to be one of the oldest spiritual symbols associated with the Celtic people, originating in the Book of

Kells, an illuminated manuscript written in the 9th century that contains the four Gospels of the New Testament, in addition to several other assorted texts and tables. The book was transcribed in Latin, but it contains various images from contemporary Ireland, Scotland, or England, including the Triquetra.

The Triskelion:

The Triskelion contains a triple spiral that represents the unity of the elements of fire, water, and earth. The name "Triskelion" stems from the Greek word "triskele," which means "three-legged." It was found in Neolithic and Bronze Age artifacts and Celtic depictions dating back from the Iron Age. Three is an important number in Celtic paganism. The Triskelion displays this with its three spiral patterns that swirl out from the center. It symbolizes progress and moving forward as an individual and a society. When the spirals are shown clockwise, it embodies a balance or harmony with nature. However, if the spirals are counter-clockwise, it is believed to assert an attempt to manipulate the natural order.

The Wicker Man:

The Wicker Man is a symbol from Celtic paganism that depicts an effigy of a large human made out of wicker, straw, and hay. The ancient Celtic people purportedly used it as a means for human or animal sacrifice. The victim would be secured within the Wicker Man, and then it would be set on fire as part of a pagan ceremony. Although there is little historical evidence to corroborate the accounts from ancient Greek and Roman sources, the Wicker Man as a symbol has endured through the years, becoming intrinsically linked with the Celtic pagans. Neopagan religions have adopted the Wicker Man in their rituals, albeit without human or animal sacrifices. They will often burn a wicker effigy as part of their Midsummer celebrations.

The Dara Celtic Knot:

The Dara Celtic Knot is an interwoven design resembling a series of crisscrossing knots in a somewhat grid-like pattern. Its name is derived from the Irish word for "oak tree," which is "doire." The symbol represents an ancient oak tree's root system, and it has no beginning or end, signifying the continuous cycles of life. The Celtic people and Druids strongly favor nature and consider oak trees sacred. It is also a symbol of strength, as the root system runs deep, allowing the tree to withstand the fury of the elements. The Dara Celtic Knot can be used for decoration. Still, it's also employed in spiritual charms and rituals performed by Druids and shamans.

The Claddagh Ring:

The Claddagh Ring is a traditional Irish ring that contains the shape of a heart and a crown clasped together. The heart is meant to represent love, and the crown represents loyalty. Having the heart clasping the crown signifies friendship. They were first produced in Galway, Ireland, during the 18th century. Still, their popularity really began to boom in the Victorian age. The use of the Claddagh Ring spread beyond the British Isles during the late 19th and 20th centuries. How the ring is worn denotes different meanings. The heart pointing toward your wrist and worn on the left hand shows that you are married, and the heart pointing to your wrist on the right hand shows that you are in a relationship. The heart pointed out on the left hand shows that you are engaged, and the heart pointed out on the right hand shows you are single.

The Ailm:

The Ailm is derived from the letter of Ogham, or the Celtic tree alphabet, which shares its name. It is traditionally believed to depict a silver fir or conifer tree. It symbolizes inner strength, resilience, endurance, purification, good health, healing, and fertility. Being a symbol from a written form of communication, the Ailm carries the connotation of wisdom and knowledge, especially that which endures from generation to generation. The Celtic people greatly revered trees, so any imagery that represents them also embodies the characteristics associated with sacred trees.

The Wheel of Taranis:

The Wheel of Taranis is a symbol associated with the thunder god Taranis, as it is one of the two items he is depicted as holding in his hands, the other being a lightning bolt. It is shown as a circle with eight spokes extending from the center, giving it the appearance of a ship's helm. It represents the eight Gaelic festivals celebrated throughout the year by Celtic pagans and neopagans (Yule, Imbolc, Ostara, Beltane, Litha, Lughnasadh, Mabon, and Samhain). The Wheel of Taranis is emblematic of the cyclical nature of the world and how it continues turning in an endless loop of birth, maturity, death, and rebirth.

The Shamrock:

The Shamrock is an Irish staple, representing good fortune and luck. Druids use it as a symbol of the triad, as it is made up of three heart-shaped leaves. The importance of the number three can be seen in much of the Celtic and Druidic iconography since there is a belief that three is a sacred number. This can also be seen in Christian imagery, as the Holy Trinity also contains three beings - the Father, the Son, and the Holy Spirit. Shamrocks are considered the national plant of Ireland, where they can be found all across the land since they thrive in cool, damp climates.

The Celtic Motherhood Knot:

The Celtic Motherhood Knot represents the strong bond between a mother and her child. Although they can have a variety of designs, most include two hearts and triquetra intertwined with each other, signifying the familial relationship and love for one another. One heart is set lower than the other, denoting the generational aspect of the mother and child. The endless love symbolized by the Celtic Motherhood Knot has also been used by Celtic pagans with Christianity influences to represent the Madonna and her son, Jesus.

The Serch Bythol:

The Serch Bythol is a symbol created by two connected triquetras. Usually, one is a slightly different shade or color from the other, denoting two separate souls joining together in a union. It represents a deep, everlasting love, a powerful reminder of the strong emotions tied to a relationship. This symbol is typically chosen to denote an engagement or marriage, but it can be used for any serious partnership. The symmetrical halves demonstrate the unification of two minds, bodies, and spirits, while the circle in the middle shows the eternal love that binds them all together.

Chapter 5: Ogham: The Celtic Tree Alphabet

Ogham (pronounced "oh-uhm") is an alphabet used by the Celtic people thousands of years ago. It is also known as the Celtic tree alphabet because each of the letters correlates to a different type of tree. The simplicity of Ogham belies its functional complexity, as most of the letters consist of basic tally marks, dashes, and a few modest shapes. However, with a few exceptions, it can usually be transposed onto the Latin alphabet like a cipher since they share many similarities.

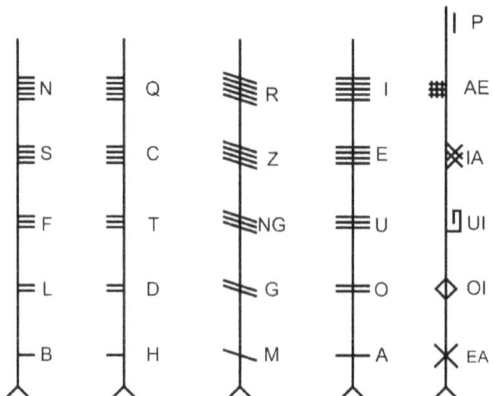

Ogham is an alphabet used by the Celtic people thousands of years ago.
Runologe, CC BY-SA 4.0 <https://creativecommons.org/licenses/by-sa/4.0>, via Wikimedia Commons: https://commons.wikimedia.org/wiki/File:All_Ogham_letters_including_Forfeda_-_%C3%9Cbersicht_aller_Ogham-Zeichen_einschlie%C3%9Flich_Forfeda.jpg

Origins of Ogham

Ogham was developed between the 1st century BCE and the 4th century AD. It was used to record the first written sources of the Archaic Irish language, including over 400 orthodox inscriptions etched upon stone monuments scattered around Ireland and western Britain. Ancient Druids created these monuments from the 4th to the 6th century, as they were most likely the only literate members of Celtic society at that time. Later, from the 6th to the 9th centuries, Ogham evolved into writing Old Irish or Old Gaelic.

Since any examples of Ogham written on wood or other perishable materials have decomposed long ago, only those inscribed on stone survive. Many of these stones are actually grave markers, and a handful contains personal names and indicators of land ownership. In Ireland, Wales, Scotland, the Isle of Man, and southwest England, the stone monuments with Ogham inscriptions have been definitively identified as territorial signs and memorials to the dead. The only one of these stones that has a name of an individual with a historical record is the memorial to Vortiporius, a Welsh king who ruled Dyfed in the 6th century.

Legendary Account of Ogham's Origins

Medieval Irish folklore credits the creation of Ogham to a mythical Scythian king named Fenius Farsa. It claims that the alphabet came about at the same time as the Gaelic language, following shortly after the destruction of the Tower of Babel in the land of Shinar when the ability to understand the universal language was stripped from humanity. Fenius trekked from his home in Scythia to the ruins of the Tower of Babel alongside Íar mac Nema, Goídel mac Ethéoir, and a group of 72 scholars. They had hoped to study the confused languages left in the wake of the tower's fall, but upon their arrival, they discovered that these languages had already been scattered across the world.

Fenius charged his scholars with going out to find and study the dispersed languages while he remained at the tower and coordinated their efforts. Ten years later, the scholars returned, having completed their assignments, and Fenius took the best parts of each confused language, establishing the "selected language." He called his new language "Goidelic" in honor of Goídel mac Ethéoir. Later, he developed an extension of Goidelic known as "Íarmberla," named for Íar mac Nema, as well as "Bérla Féne," which was named after himself. Finally, he perfected his language's writing system, dubbing it "Beithe-luis-nuin," otherwise known as "Ogham." Supposedly, the names of the letters in Ogham are that of his 25 best scholars.

Another legend ascribes the creation of Ogham to the god Oghma. He was said to be a skilled speaker and poet, having the ability to be very persuasive. His reasoning for developing this alphabet was to exclude any fools or rustic people, only wanting to associate with learned individuals. The first message written by Oghma in his new system was a series of seven b's on a piece of wood from a birch. This was meant to be a warning to his fellow god, Lugh, cautioning him that his wife would be stolen away seven times to the Otherworld unless he protected her with the birch. For this reason, the letter b in Ogham was named for the birch, and tradition holds that the other letters were given names after trees as well.

Purpose of Ogham

Two main theories have been proposed about why the Ogham was created. Scholars are split as to which theory they believe is correct, and there hasn't been a general consensus in favor of one over the other. Until more relics or artifacts containing Ogham are found, it's impossible to determine for certain which theory carries more weight. At this time, both have their merits, but they also have their detractors, as modern academia cannot account for all the missing information that would sway the minds of those who study Ogham.

Theory #1

The first theory is that the language was invented to serve as a cryptic alphabet, preventing anyone who is only familiar with the Latin alphabet from being able to decipher this writing. Ancient Druids could have used Ogham as a secret method of communication between Celtic tribes. They would have been able to talk about politics, military operations, intelligence gathering, and religion without fear of being exposed if their correspondences were intercepted. This was a particularly dangerous time for the Celtic people living in the British Isles, as they had to ensure the Romans occupying Britain did not discover their communications. There was a serious fear in Ireland that the Romans might invade their home next, and they wanted to be ready for any potential conflict in the future.

Centuries later, when the people of Ireland had launched their own invasion of western Britain, it would have continued to be useful for them to maintain the secrecy of their communications from the Romans or Romano-Britons that remained in the region. This is where the theory runs into some trouble. By this point, there were inscriptions in Wales that used Ogham and Latin together. Literacy had increased enough in the post-Roman British Isles that it would have been easy enough for any messages coded in Ogham to be deciphered, making it difficult to keep any plans from reaching their enemies.

Theory #2

The second theory is that Ogham was developed by the earliest Christian communities that arose in Ireland to have a unique alphabet when composing short inscriptions or messages in the Irish language. Archaic Irish included vocalized sounds that would have been difficult to transcribe using the Latin alphabet, necessitating the creation of a separate system. There was known to be a community of Christians living in Ireland in about 400 AD, whose existence was documented by Prosper of Aquitaine in the Universal Chronicle. Writing in 431 AD, prosper recounted the mission of Palladius, Bishop of Ireland, who was sent there by Pope Celestine I.

In the 4th century, Irish settlements appeared in the western parts of Wales. It is believed that a variation of Ogham was established here after the settlers intermingled with the Romano-Britons, who were well-versed in the Latin alphabet. This would explain the stone monuments found in Wales that contain both Ogham and Latin inscriptions. While it makes sense that these stones may have been the result of contact between Irish Christians and Romanized Britons, there is a lack of direct evidence concerning the creators of the Welsh stone monuments to prove this theory true.

Debunked Theory

There was originally a third theory that had previously been a part of Ogham scholarship, but it fell out of favor as studies of the language evolved to include more comprehensive examinations of the relationship between the culture and writings. This theory proposed that Druids living in Cisalpine Gaul around 600 BCE had concocted a secret system of hand and finger signals inspired by a variation of the Greek alphabet contemporaneous to Northern Italy. These hand signals were later transcribed through oral accounts or on wooden materials, making their way with the ancient Celts when they arrived in the British Isles. Eventually, this system was inscribed on the stone monuments during the days of the early Christians in Ireland.

This theory was debunked because later detailed studies proved Ogham was developed specifically for Archaic Irish during the earliest centuries AD. Any connection to the Greek alphabet has also been disproved, with there being only superficial commonalities between the two writing systems that do not hold up to deeper scrutiny. Modern scholars have almost unanimously rejected the theory as a viable interpretation of the origins of Ogham. The only part of the theory that has any relevance is the idea that the hand or finger signals were reflected through the use of tally marks to form the Ogham script.

Composition of Ogham

The individual letters that make up Ogham consist of 25 characters. They are based on tally marks, dashes, and basic symbols. Each character is assigned a corresponding value in the Latin alphabet, usually derived from the name of the Ogham letter in Archaic or Old Irish. Originally, there were only 20 characters, but 5 more were added over the centuries, bringing the total to 25. It is believed that the Ogham script was inspired by a counting system that predates the Celtic tree alphabet, based around the numbers 5 and 20. This system was then adapted by the first Oghamists.

Letters of Ogham

b—Beith (Old Irish: Beithe): Beith translates to "birch," which is also the tree associated with it in the arboreal tradition.

l—Luis (Old Irish: Luis): Luis translates to either "herb" or "flame." In the arboreal tradition, it is associated with "mountain-ash," also known as rowan.

w—Fearn (Old Irish: Fern): Fearn translates to "alder-tree," which is why it is associated with alder in the arboreal tradition. In Archaic Irish, it was spelled "wernā," which is why it has been ascribed the letter "w."

s—Sail (Old Irish: Sail): Sail translates to "willow," which is also the tree associated with it in the arboreal tradition.

n—Nion (Old Irish: Nin): Nion translates to "forked branch" or "loftiness." In the arboreal tradition, it is associated with ash.

j—Uath (Old Irish: Úath): Uath translates to "fear" or "horror." In the arboreal tradition, it is associated with "white-thorn," also known as hawthorn. The reason it has been ascribed the letter "j" is unclear as its original etymology is not known.

d—Dair (Old Irish: Dair): Dair translates to "oak," which is also the tree associated with it in the arboreal tradition.

t—Tinne (Old Irish: Tinne): Tinne translates to "iron bar" or "ingot." In the arboreal tradition, it is associated with holly.

k—Coll (Old Irish: Coll): Coll translates to "fair-wood" or "hazel-tree," which is why it is associated with hazel in the arboreal tradition.

kw—Ceirt (Old Irish: Cert): Ceirt translates to "fair" or "just." In the arboreal tradition, it is associated with apple trees.

m—Muin (Old Irish: Muin): Muin translates to "neck," "trick," or "esteem." In the arboreal tradition, it is associated with thickets of thorns. It is often mistakenly assigned an association with grape vines, but as grapes have never been successfully cultivated or grown in Ireland, this is an erroneous attribution.

g—Gort (Old Irish: Gort): Gort translates to "field" or "garden." In the arboreal tradition, it is associated with ivy.

gw—nGéadal (Old Irish: Gétal): nGéadal translates to the verbs "to wound" or "to stab." In the arboreal tradition, it is associated with a fern or broom. This letter's original phonetic value in Archaic Irish was "gw," the voiced labiovelar. This phoneme was merged with "g" (gort) in Old Irish, and medieval manuscripts assigned it the Latin letter "ng" (ŋ), which is why "nGéadal" is spelled with the initial "n-."

st—Straif (Old Irish: Straiph): Straif translates to "sulfur." In the arboreal tradition, it is associated with blackthorn.

r—Ruis (Old Irish: Ruis): Ruis translates to "red" or "reddening." In the arboreal tradition, it is associated with elderberries due to the practice of using the juice extracted from the berries to redden the cheeks.

a—Ailm (Old Irish: Ailm): Ailm's original translation cannot be definitely established, but some etymologists believe it is meant to represent a groan. In the arboreal tradition, it is associated with silver fir and conifer trees, or possibly pine trees.

o—Onn (Old Irish: Onn) Onn translates to "ash-tree," which is why it is associated with ash in the arboreal tradition.

u—Úr (Old Irish: Úr): Úr translates to "earth," "soil," "clay," "moist," and "fresh." In the arboreal tradition, it is associated with heather.

e—Eadhadh (Old Irish: Edad): Eadhadh has no known translation, but in the arboreal tradition, it is associated with "true-tree" or aspen.

i—Iodhadh (Old Irish: Idad): Iodhadh is sometimes translated as "yew," which is also the tree associated with it in the arboreal tradition.

The following letters are known as the "forfeda," which are additional letters added to the basic 20 signs of Ogham:

ea—Éabhadh (Old Irish: Ébhadh): Éabhadh has no known translation, but in the arboreal tradition, it is associated with aspen. It is also sometimes paired with Eadhadh, which is associated with the same tree.

oi—Ór (Old Irish: Óir): Ór translates to "gold." In the arboreal tradition, it is associated with "spindle-tree" or ivy.

ui—Uilleann (Old Irish: Uilleand): Uilleann translates to "elbow." In the arboreal tradition, it is associated with honeysuckle.

p/io—Pín/Peithe/Ifín (Old Irish: Pín/Peithe/Iphín): The letter Pín was added to Ogham several centuries after its creation since Archaic Irish did not have a "p." Later on, certain scholars believed the forfeda were all vowels, they added the letter Peithe, reassigning "p" from Pín to Peithe, which was pronounced with a soft "p," or "ph-" sound. The letter Ifín was given the value of "io" to account for this change. In the arboreal tradition, it is associated with gooseberries or thorns.

x/ai—Eamhancholl (Old Irish: Emancholl): Eamhancholl translates to "twins of coll" or "twins of hazel." Like the letter coll, it is associated with hazel in the arboreal tradition.

Chart of Ogham Characters

┬ Beith (*b*)	┬┬ Luis (*l*)	┬┬┬ Fearn (*w*)	┬┬┬┬ Sail (*s*)	┬┬┬┬┬ Nion (*n*)
┴ Uath (*y*)	┴┴ Dair (*d*)	┴┴┴ Tinne (*t*)	┴┴┴┴ Coll (*k*)	┴┴┴┴┴ Ceirt (*kʷ*)
╱ Muin (*m*)	╱╱ Gort (*g*)	╱╱╱ nGéadal (*gʷ*)	╱╱╱╱ Straif (*st*)	╱╱╱╱╱ Ruis (*r*)
· Ailm (*a*)	·· Onn (*o*)	··· Úr (*u*)	···· Eadhadh (*e*)	····· Iodhadh (*i*)
✳ Éabhadh (*ea*)	◊ Ór (*oi*)	⊡ Uilleann (*ui*)	−/✕ Peithe/Ifín (*p/io*)	▦ Eamhancholl (*x/ai*)

Ogham Ciphers

When writing with Ogham, you can indicate the start and end of a sentence or phrase through the use of feather marks that look like this: ⟩⟨

The Ogham characters go in between, all running along a single horizontal line (Ogham can be written vertically as well, but it's much easier for those familiar with any languages that are written and read from left to right to use the horizontal configuration), leaving spaces between them to indicate the separation of words. For example, if you wanted to write "This is a cipher," here's how it would look in Ogham:

The phrase opens with a feather mark and then uses the characters Tinne (t), Uath (j), Iodhadh (i), Sail (s); Iodhadh (i), Sail (s); Ailm (a); Coll (k), Iodhadh (i), Peithe (p), Uath (j), Eadhadh (e), Ruis (r). It then ends with another feather mark. Note that the translation from English to Ogham is not a perfect 1:1, since they do not have all the same letters. The Uath's "j" is substituted for "h," and the Coll's "k" replaces the "c." In the former's instance, despite being written with a "j," Uath usually functions as an "h," and the latter case uses a "k" for the "c" because the letter "c" is only pronounced as a hard "c," or a "k" sound, rather than varying between a hard and soft "c" like in English.

To create an Ogham cipher by translating English to Ogham and vice versa, some letters from Ogham will be reused for more than one letter in English, while some are not used except under specific conditions. You can refer to the chart below for the basic translations from Ogham to the Latin alphabet:

a	B	c/k	d
e	f/w*	g	h/j**
i	j/i***	k	l
m	N	o	p
q/kʷ	R	s	t
u	v/w****	w	x

⌗ y/gʷ	⫽ z/st		

*Since there is no equivalent for the Latin letter "f," it uses Fearn, as the "w" of Fearn is normally pronounced like a Latin "v."

**While Uath is represented by the letter "j," it is normally pronounced as if it was a Latin letter "h."

***Even though Uath is represented by the letter "j," it is not the equivalent of "j" in the Latin alphabet. Instead, the Latin Letter "j" uses Iodhadh, the same as the letter "i."

****There is no difference between the Latin "v" and "w" in Ogham, so both use the "w" of Fearn.

⌗

⫽

Ogham Cipher Exercises

See if you can decipher the following sentences encoded using Ogham:

〉╫╫ ╫╫ ━•╥━╫╫ •╥ ╫╫╫•╫╥╫╫ ━╥╥ ┆ ╥╥ ╥╥ ━•╥━╫╫〈

Decoded: _
_ _ _ .

〉╥━╫╫╫ ╫╫╫━╫ ━•╥━╫╫╫╫•/━╥ ╫╫╫━╫╫╫━╥━•╥╥╥┬━╥╥╫〈

Decoded: _
_ _ _ _ _ _ _ .

〉╫╫━•╥╥╫╫╫╫━╥╥╫╥ •╥┆╥ ╥•╥━╫╫╥╥━╫╫━╫╥╥╥〈

Decoded: _
_ _ _ _ _ _ _ _ _ _ _ _ .

Answers:
1. "By the power of Grayskull, I have the power." [b(y/gʷ) t(h/j)e power o(f/w) gra(y/gʷ)skull i (h/j)a(v/w)e the power]
2. "With great power comes great responsibility." [wit(h/j) great power (c/k)omes great responsibilit(y/gʷ)]
3. "The only thing we have to fear is fear itself." [t(h/j)e onl(y/gʷ) t(h/j)ing we (h/j)a(v/w)e to (f/w)ear is (f/w)ear itsel(f/w)]

Chapter 6: Druidic Tree Astrology

Druidic Tree Astrology, also known as Celtic Tree Astrology, is a divinatory practice based on the beliefs of the ancient Druids. They maintained that the date and time a person was born was a significant aspect of how their personality formed. Because of this, the Druids made predictions as to what types of characteristics a person would develop as they matured into an adult.

Trees of Celtic Astrology

Birch

Birch Tree.
https://pixabay.com/es/photos/paisaje-abedules-%c3%a1rboles-lago-agua-2577207/

Title: The Achiever
Birthdates: December 24 to January 20
Traits: Loving, Ambitious, Courageous
Compatibility: Willow and Vine

You are a highly driven individual, possessing the capability to motivate other people. When a crisis arises, you will step forward to take charge of the situation, but you make sure to do it while keeping in mind the feelings and emotions of others. Because of your ambitious and determined nature, you seek ways to acquire knowledge and learn as much as possible. Your resilience in the face of adversity is evident, and despite your versatility, you are always striving for more. You can be quick-witted and charming, making friends easily and able to put a smile on people's faces.

Exercise to Try: Red Crane Focus Meditation

The red crane focus meditation technique is a great way to find balance in your life. Like the red crane that balances itself on one leg, you will be able to equally distribute your responsibilities and desires so that one doesn't outweigh the other. Keeping your life in harmony is important to remain happy and healthy. There are many things that meditation can help you with, including easing tension and ridding yourself of stress. This technique will grant you the serenity you deserve so that you can focus on the important things in life.

How to Do It:

1. Start by finding a place to sit. Make sure that you're comfortable. You can sit cross-legged or place the soles of your feet together, letting your knees fall to the side.
2. Close your eyes and begin to count while breathing. Inhale through your nose, counting to 4 as you fill your lungs with air.
3. Hold your breath while counting to 7. Visualize all your problems and stress being gathered into one place as if you were balling up a wad of paper.
4. Exhale through your mouth while counting to 8. Your breath out should be audible, making a whooshing sound. Picture that ball of problems and stress being blown out of your both, expelling it all from your body.

5. Repeat the 4-7-8 breathing technique 5 times, cleansing your body of any negative energy.
6. Relax the muscles in your jaw and face. Drop your shoulders and allow your hands and arms to go limp. Feel the muscles in your legs and feet relax as well. You should be completely at ease once you are through.
7. Visualize everything you need to take care of for the day, and then think about something you want to do for fun. Imagine them sitting on opposite sides of a scale. As you focus on balancing the scale, remind yourself that once you have fulfilled your responsibilities, you will allow yourself time to do something you enjoy.
8. Return your focus to your breathing and repeat the 4-7-8 technique for 5 more repetitions. On your final exhale, open your eyes. You should now have a clearer picture of how to go about your day while balancing your duties with your desires.

Rowan

Rowan Tree.
https://pixabay.com/es/photos/serbal-bayas-sorbus-planta-%c3%a1rbol-3571546/

Title: The Thinker

Birthdates: January 21 to February 17

Traits: Intelligent, Patient, Influential

Compatibility: Hawthorn and Ivy

You are the kind of person who has a clear vision of what you want, and you tend to set lofty goals for yourself. While appearing calm on the outside, there is a constant rush of energy on the inside that helps to inspire you. You have a great imagination and unique ideas, which can sometimes intimidate others. Your fierce nature and hardened exterior hide a patient, kind, and caring heart. Your capacity to improve your circumstances and those around you through a sharp, compassionate mind often prove a great boon to other people. While you may appear reserved, your silent determination draws people toward you.

Exercise to Try: Whispered Stillness Guided ASMR Meditation

Everyone who meditates has the goal of finding stillness during their exercises. Using a whispered stillness-guided ASMR meditation can lead you down that path, guiding you the whole way as your body and mind achieve the stillness you desire. ASMR can offer a soothing retreat from the chaos of the world around you, and hearing the sleep-inducing whispers from a calming voice can offer you a deep sense of serenity. The stillness will slowly wash over you until every part of you is completely relaxed, aiding you in drifting off to a restive and restorative sleep.

How to Do It:

Find a whispered stillness-guided ASMR meditation track on an audio website or app like Spotify, or use a video from YouTube. Allow the guided meditation to play from your smartphone or another electronic device, and close your eyes, following the instructions as you are guided to sleep.

Ash

Ash Tree.
https://pixabay.com/es/photos/fraxinus-excelsior-ceniza-844653/

Title: The Enchanter
Birthdates: February 18 to March 17
Traits: Artistic, Imaginative, Open-Minded, Independent
Compatibility: Reed and Willow

You have a fantastic personality that many people find enticing, but your shy nature means you prefer to spend plenty of time alone. The beauty of nature inspires you, and your creativity is seemingly boundless. The subjects that most interest you include art, science, writing, poetry, and spirituality. While others might view you as a bit of a recluse, you don't mind, as you have no problem immersing yourself in your own inner world of wonder and imagination. You constantly reinvent yourself and strive to do whatever makes you happy, regardless of what other people might think. Because of your creativity and independence, you inspire those around you to seek their own happiness.

Exercise to Try: Relaxing Early Morning Ocean Breath Meditation

You can tap into the calming power of ocean breath meditation early in the morning to aid you in getting your day started on the right foot. Relaxation will flow through you, washing away the tension and frustration that you might face at home, work, school, or just out in the world. Beginning the day with ocean breath meditation can stick with you all the way into the evening, keeping you centered and balanced for any curveballs life might throw at you.

How to Do It:

1. Sit up tall, close your eyes, and allow your shoulders to relax away from your ears. In preparation for this meditation, focus on your breathing without trying to control it. Start to inhale and exhale through your mouth instead of your nose.
2. Move your focus to your throat. When you exhale, try to tone the back of your throat (your glottis or soft palate). The goal is to slightly constrict the air passage. If you're having trouble with this, think of the way you fog up a pane of glass. There should be a soft hissing or wheezing sound.
3. When you are comfortable with this type of exhale, apply the same throat contraction to your inhalation. You should hear the same soft hissing or wheezing sound as you breathe. The name of this breathing technique is derived from that sound, as it

resembles the sounds of the ocean. If you are a fan of "Star Wars," you might call it Darth Vader Meditation since it also sounds like his iconic breathing.

4. Once you have full control of your throat while inhaling and exhaling, close your mouth and start breathing through your nose. Continue to apply the same toning to your throat as you did when you were breathing through your mouth. Your breaths will continue to make a similar noise as it moves in and out through your nose.

5. Breathe like this for about five minutes, using each exhale to push any intrusive thoughts out of your mind. This is a time to allow total relaxation to wash over your body, so you must empty your mind. It may help to focus your attention on your breathing, imagining that you are sitting on a beach near the seashore, listening to the ocean as it ebbs and flows.

Alder

Alder Tree.
https://pixabay.com/es/photos/del-aliso-negro-blackle-4681232/

Title: The Trailblazer

Birthdates: March 18 to April 14

Traits: Brave, Romantic, Generous

Compatibility: Birch and Oak

You are always on the move, and you dislike wasting time on superficiality. Positive energy about you is constantly projected out, drawing people toward you. You are also a natural leader, falling comfortably into the role even when you don't intend to take charge. There is an easy-going charm about you, and as an extrovert, you never have trouble mingling with a crowd, no matter what types of personalities are present. Your knack for getting along with everyone means people enjoy being in your company. There is an attractiveness to your self-confidence, making you seem irresistible to others. You have a passionate heart and aren't afraid to share it with those you care about.

Exercise to Try: Breath of Fire Meditation

Wake up with a breath of fire meditation, giving you the boost you need without resorting to filling your body with toxins like caffeine. Yogis have taught this method of meditation for thousands of years, and the results speak for themselves. Your energy levels and productivity will increase, allowing you to tackle your challenges. Having a means of natural stimulation is a healthier alternative to artificial stimulants, and you'll feel stronger, clearer, and more powerful than those who have to depend on other means of getting their energy for the day.

How to Do It:

1. Begin by sitting in a cross-legged position. Make sure to sit up tall.
2. Place your hands on your knees with your palms facing upward. You can also place a hand on your belly, feeling it rise and fall as you breathe.
3. Inhale through your nose, allowing your belly to expand as you breathe in.
4. Without pausing, exhale forcefully through your nose, contracting your abdominal muscles as you do. Make sure the length of time you breathe in is the same as when you breathe out. Repeat this pattern until you become comfortable with it.
5. Maintain this rhythm, inhaling slowly and exhaling forcefully. Continue to repeat these actions multiple times for practice.
6. Next, speed up your breathing, inhaling and exhaling faster. Remember, your exhales should still be forceful and loud.
7. Repeat the faster breathing for 30 seconds.

Over time, as you become more accustomed to using the Breath of Fire breathing technique, you can try to do it for longer periods.

Willow

Willow Tree.
https://pixabay.com/es/photos/%c3%a1rbol-estanque-sauce-naturaleza-984846/

Title: The Observer

Birthdates: April 15 to May 12

Traits: Intuitive, Sympathetic, Calm

Compatibility: Ivy and Birch

You are someone who values honesty and integrity. Your sympathetic and generous nature is often on display since you are the type of person who prefers peace and love to drama and chaos. Not only are you intellectual, but you also have a great amount of emotional intelligence, capable of understanding how those around you are feeling, even if they don't tell you. You have a grounded perspective on life, seeing the reality of a situation but never resorting to cynicism. When dealing with others, you are extremely polite and kind. However, you also enjoy joking around with your friends and have a great sense of humor. When people are around you, they can't help but be cheered up and see the brighter side of things.

Exercise to Try: State of Stillness Meditation

Using the state of stillness meditation is a great remedy for anyone with difficulty sleeping. Spend the night tossing and turning, unable to calm your mind and relax your body. You can use this technique to grant you the peace necessary for a proper period of rest. This form of guided meditation will induce a state of stillness and relaxation that will ease your mind and release the tension from your body. Once you are able to drift off, you'll find yourself in a deep, unburdened sleep, enjoying the restoration granted by having a night of uninterrupted slumber. This will allow your mind and body to recover, ready to face the morning when you finally awaken.

How to Do It:

1. Lie down on your bed and find a comfortable position. Extend your legs out and allow your arms to rest alongside your body, turning your palms to face up.
2. Begin by scrunching and tightening your feet and toes, then relax them. Your muscles should contract and release. Do this multiple times, working any tension out of your feet.
3. Again, tighten your feet and toes as you inhale deeply, and then relax as you fully exhale.
4. Moving up your body, repeat the technique of contracting and releasing your muscles. Do it with your ankles, your legs, your hips and rear, your belly, your chest, your hands, your arms, your shoulders, your neck, and your face. Remember to continue with your breathing as you do this.
5. Complete three repetitions of tightening and relaxing your whole body.
6. After the final repetition, close your eyes, contracting every muscle in your body as you inhale. Upon exhaling, release your muscles, pushing out all the tension. Return your breathing to normal, and you should be able to fall asleep peacefully.

Hawthorn

Hawthorn Tree.
https://pixabay.com/es/photos/espino-floraci%c3%b3n-%c3%a1rbol-wet-4196348/

Title: The Illusionist
Birthdates: May 13 to June 9
Traits: Passionate, Fun, Secretive, Wily
Compatibility: Rowan and Ash

You are a person who has a lot more going on inside than you allow people to see. There is a great amount of passion and creativity within you; you are just searching for a constructive outlet. You tend to see the big picture, which grants you the ability to adapt to nearly any situation. It also lets you display a sense of maturity that shows you are intelligent and even-tempered. You're a naturally curious person, always seeking to learn new things. This makes you a great listener, and people feel comfortable divulging their deepest secrets. You have an ironic sense of humor, often picking up on subtleties and making insightful observations. However, this may be veiled in the form of jokes.

Exercise to Try: Fast Asleep Meditation Technique

The fast-asleep meditation technique helps to slow down a busy mind and helps you get to sleep quickly. You have plenty of responsibilities to take care of every single day, and you can't afford to waste a single moment of the night lying awake in bed, unable to push out the mental to-do lists or instinctive planning for the following morning. This meditation technique can help slow the chaos running through your head, allowing you to fall asleep fast. Maximizing the limited time you have to rest makes you more likely to wake up feeling refreshed.

How to Do It:

Start by scanning your body. This means taking notice of your breathing and the spots where your body is in contact with your bed. Beginning with your toes, mentally "turn off" any tension or movement in that part of your body. Let them go limp and keep them relaxed. Repeat this process for each part of your body, from the tips of your toes to the top of your head.

Begin counting your breaths as they alternate between inhales and exhales. Start by counting the first breath in as 1, then the following breath out as 2. When you inhale again, count 3; when you exhale, count 4. Continue doing this until you get to 10. This is to keep your focus on your breathing, allowing all other thoughts to melt away. If your mind wanders to other things, restart your counting at 1.

Oak

Oak Tree.
https://pixabay.com/es/photos/roble-%c3%a1rbol-bosque-prado-oto%c3%b1o-7468708/

Title: The Stabilizer

Birthdates: June 10 to July 7

Traits: Loyal, Peaceful, Courageous, Fair-Minded

Compatibility: Reed and Ash

You are someone who feels strongly about defending those who cannot speak up for themselves, acting as a champion of righteousness. Your sympathies will almost always lie with the underdog, as you believe they should be given a fair shot in life. Due to this, many people want to be your friend, and you have a large social network. There is a calming effect about your presence, as people feel safe and comfortable around you. You have great respect for history, using your knowledge of the past to gain insight into the future. Whenever you get a chance to spend time with your friends and family, you have a great time reminiscing with everyone.

Exercise to Try: Healing Waters Meditation

You can use the power of healing waters meditation to visualize and release any mental, emotional, or physical pain you are carrying. Anxiety, sadness, anger, and tension build up throughout the day, causing you to bear that weight as you attempt to go about your routine. Fortunately, the purifying relief of the healing waters technique will wash over you and flush that weight from your mind, body, and spirit.

How to Do It:

Find a comfortable place to sit down. You can then use an audio track or video guiding you through healing waters meditation, repeating the mantra when prompted and following the instructions, or you can read them to yourself. For the latter option, the following will serve as your guide:

(Speak out loud)

"I shall let the water soothe me and heal my pain in my mind, my body, and my soul. I have brought it all here right now so the healing waters can wash it away."

1. Settle your body and find your breath. Wiggle around a bit to release any tension and make yourself comfortable.
2. The next time you exhale, allow your shoulders to drop and relax your body.
3. Breathe in and out. Each time you do this, extend your breaths a little longer and breathe in a bit deeper.
4. Draw out the breaths and slow them down. Try to slow down your mind and your body as well.
5. Take a pause.
6. If you can feel any physical pain, try to pinpoint its origin. Visualize a warm hum being emitted from that spot.
7. Say out loud, *"This is my pain, and I reject it. Where there was pain, I feel only the healing energy of the sea."*
8. If you feel pain in your heart or mind, allow yourself to experience it at the moment. Do not cling to it; release it from you.
9. • (Say out loud, *"This is my pain, and I have set it free. Where there was pain, I feel only the rejuvenating power of the ocean."*
10. Take a pause.
11. Listen carefully for the sound of the water all around you. Picture the waves of the ocean racing across the sand, and then see them retreat back to the sea.
12. As you breathe in, imagine the waves washing through you. As you breathe out, imagine them ebbing and taking your pain with them back to the sea.

Holly

Holly Tree.
https://pixabay.com/es/photos/holly-tree-houx-stechpalme-acebo-1030595/

Title: The Ruler

Birthdates: July 8 to August 4

Traits: Leader, Confident, Noble

Compatibility: Elder and Ash

You have an air of nobility about you, and others view you as a respectable person. You are often looked to by others to provide leadership, and your natural confidence allows you to take on the mantle of leadership without hesitation. Failure is not an option for you, and you press forth when faced with obstacles, finding new and inventive ways to overcome them. In the rare instance that you experience a setback, it only spurs you on to work harder and refocus your efforts on reaching your objective. You are organized and goal-oriented even when spending your time on leisurely activities. This can be intimidating to outsiders, but those within your inner circle know that you are also a warm and generous person.

Exercise to Try: Mindfulness Meditation

Mindfulness meditation can help you be fully present in the moment. You should always take some time to focus on where you are and what you're doing in the here and now rather than thinking about the past or the future. This prevents you from becoming overwhelmed by your responsibilities or the drama in your life. The more you worry about other things while going about your normal routine, the greater the chance that something slips your mind or you make a mistake that could've been avoided if you'd been paying closer attention. Take notice of your thoughts, emotions, and senses as you are currently experiencing them.

How to Do It:

1. Take a seat. Find a place that offers a stable, solid surface. This can be a chair, a bench, a cushion, or anything else, as long as you're not perching or hanging back.
2. Observe what your legs are doing. If you're on a cushion or sitting on the floor, comfortably cross your legs in front of you. If you are experienced with any seated yoga postures, use those instead. If you're sitting on a chair, bench, or other raised surface, make sure the soles of your feet are touching the floor.
3. Straighten your upper body. Don't stiffen up, though. The spine has natural curvature to it, so allow it to be there. Let your head and shoulders rest on top of your vertebrae comfortably.
4. Position your upper arms parallel to your upper body. Then allow your hands to drop onto the tops of your legs. Don't try to force them into the right spot; as long as your upper arms are at your sides, your hands should naturally land correctly in your lap. If you rest them too far forward, it will cause you to hunch. If you rest them too far back, it will make you stiff. Imagine you're tuning the strings of an instrument; they shouldn't be too tight or too loose.
5. Drop your chin a bit and gently allow your gaze to fall downward. You can lower your eyelids. Should you feel the need, you can close them completely, but it's not necessary to do this while meditating. You can just let whatever your eyes are looking at remain there, focusing on it.
6. Remain in this position for a few moments. Relax and pay attention to your breathing or the sensations you feel within your body.
7. Follow your breath and feel it as it moves in and out. If you want, you can emphasize exhaling more and leave a brief pause after inhaling. Draw your attention to the actual physical sensation of breathing. Feel the air passing through your nose or mouth and the rise and fall of your belly or chest. Pick a focal point, and as you take each breath, make a mental note when you breathe in and breathe out.

8. Your mind may wander from your breathing and go to other places. That's okay. It's not necessary to block out your thoughts or eliminate them from your head. Whenever you catch your mind wandering, be it for a few seconds or a few minutes, simply return your attention to your breathing.
9. Practice taking a pause before making any physical adjustments, like if you need to move to avoid a cramp or scratch an irritating itch. You can then shift at whatever moment you choose, allowing for some space between what you are experiencing and when you take deliberate action.
10. If you find your mind is constantly wandering, that's okay, too. Rather than grappling with or engaging those thoughts, practice observing them without the need to react. Just sit there and pay attention to your breathing. It might be difficult to keep returning your attention to only your breathing, but that's all there is to do. Come back to it as often as necessary without judgments or expectations.
11. Whenever you're ready, lift your gaze back up, and open your eyes if they are closed. Take a second to listen for any sounds in the environment around you. Pay attention to how your body feels at this very moment. Pay attention to your thoughts and emotions. Before standing up, allow yourself a minute to decide how you'd like to approach the rest of your day.

Hazel

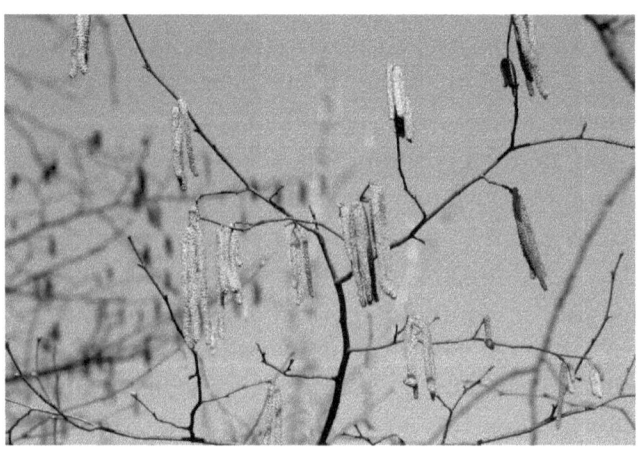

Hazel Tree.
https://pixabay.com/es/photos/color-avellana-%c3%a1rbol-rama-figura-4837464/

Title: The Knower

Birthdates: August 5 to September 1

Traits: Intelligent, Loyal, Confident

Compatibility: Rowan and Hawthorn

You tend to be introverted, preferring quiet solitude to loud social settings. However, you also have a great personality, which people find very attractive once they get to know you. You are a voracious reader, and you keep up with current events, making you a reliable information source. Since you are very intelligent, you can often figure out the best course of action to take in any given situation, but you are never conceited about your capabilities. You are fiercely loyal to your loved ones and will go to the ends of the Earth to protect them. Despite your success, you are always willing to improve yourself, acknowledging your faults and working to be a better person.

Exercise to Try: De-stressing Meditation

De-stressing meditation is a short yet efficient method for centering yourself. Try using it before going to an event you've been dreading or after a long, stressful day. No matter how minor things that irritate or upset you might seem, they can accumulate over time, snowballing into a massive weight that crashes into you and knocks you off your feet. Fortunately, de-stressing meditation can help you get through whatever challenges stand in your way. You can overcome any obstacles by keeping a clear head and a light heart.

How to Do It:

1. Get into a position that's comfortable for you. Decide where and how you will sit. Some people prefer sitting in a chair, and others like to sit cross-legged on the floor or another large, flat surface. Wherever you choose, you should be somewhere where you can fully relax while remaining alert and aware.
2. Make sure you are using the correct posture. Sitting up straight is easier to stay awake during extended meditation sessions. Suppose you remember to start each session by first adopting the correct posture. In that case, your body will become accustomed to naturally sitting in this position as you advance to spending long periods meditating.
3. During a meditation session, try to remain mindful that you maintain the correct posture. If you notice that you're slumping

your shoulders, take the opportunity to make corrections and sit back up straight. Keeping your body from using incorrect posture helps to prevent unnecessary soreness after extended meditation.

4. If you decide to sit in a chair, position yourself toward the front of the seat, and plant both feet firmly on the floor. This helps with improving your posture and allows you to concentrate on your meditation practice.

5. Once in a comfortable position, cast your gaze into the distance and lower your eyelids, but don't close your eyes yet. Your jaw should remain slack as you do this. Relax the muscles in your face while your eyes remain slightly open. After relaxing your facial muscles, you can close your eyes to begin meditating. Don't squeeze them shut tight, though. If you feel the muscles in your face tense up, slowly reopen your eyes and repeat the relaxation of your face before closing them again.

6. At this point in your meditation session, the goal is to relax every part of your body. You may feel tension in areas that tend to get tight, so take a deep breath in, hold it for a count of five seconds, and then breathe out slowly, allowing your body to relax completely.

7. Try to set your thoughts aside. Don't try to control the thoughts themselves; instead, control how much power you give them. There's no need to ignore or suppress your thoughts, but try to remain calm, take note of them, and then focus on your breathing to help you return to the moment. This practice isn't merely useful for meditation; it can aid you throughout the day, teaching you how to let things go and remain focused on the task at hand.

8. Don't become too flustered if you find your thoughts running out of control. There is no judgment here. Simply take the time to observe that you let your thoughts carry you away, and then refocus and return to your breathing. Continue to put aside any thoughts that may pop into your head. The longer you practice, the more time will pass when your mind remains quiet before your thoughts return.

9. Remember to give yourself time to adjust to your meditation practice. Don't put too much pressure on yourself to get

everything right, as this can end up causing you more stress than it relieves. It's unreasonable to expect that your meditation sessions will all be perfect. Putting yourself under that kind of pressure can make meditation feel like a chore, and it'll be less likely that you'll want to continue with it in the future.

10. Try starting with shorter 5-minute meditation sessions and slowly work your way up to longer ones. When you feel like you've gotten the hang of the 5-minute sessions, you can try doing a 10-minute session. Then move on to a 15-minute session. Keep adding another 5 minutes until you can meditate regularly for 30-minute sessions.

11. The more you practice your meditation, the easier it becomes, and it can be an effective stress relief tool. You should emerge from a 30-minute meditation session feeling refreshed, relaxed, and rejuvenated. If you meditate in the morning, you'll be ready to start your day with plenty of energy, and if you meditate at night, it will allow you to let go of the tension so you can fall asleep without a struggle.

12. It can be a good idea to set goals for yourself while meditating and keeping track of your time. If you're not used to emptying your mind and relaxing, every minute that passes might feel like an eternity, even when you've barely started the session. Constantly thinking about how much time has passed can become distracting, and if you're worrying about meditating for too long, it'll defeat the purpose of trying to de-stress.

13. The best way to handle this is to set a timer so you can be confident that you won't throw off your entire schedule. You can also play some soothing sounds or gentle music to help get you into the right headspace for meditating. This can also aid you in avoiding too many intrusive thoughts, as you can focus on the music if tracking your breathing isn't helping. Eventually, you'll get to the point where you won't need the timer, as your body will naturally become accustomed to relaxing for a set amount of time.

Vine

Vine Tree.
https://pixabay.com/es/photos/uvas-fruta-vino-planta-vid-1696921/

Title: The Equalizer

Birthdates: September 2 to September 29

Traits: Charming, Elegant, Loving

Compatibility: Willow and Hazel

You are someone who enjoys the finer things in life, never hesitant to indulge in luxuries. At the same time, you are also very generous, spreading your good fortune so others can enjoy life with you. You never expect to have things handed to you, and you are always willing to work hard to pay for your expensive tastes. Your compassionate nature means you can often see things from other people's perspectives, but this can also make you a bit unpredictable and indecisive since you will believe that both sides have a point. You also don't like conflict or confrontation, preferring to remain neutral in such situations. Although you can become withdrawn if someone breaks your heart, you always conduct yourself with poise and charm.

Exercise to Try: Beauty Sleep Meditation

The beauty sleep meditation is meant to help you enter a state of deep relaxation. It will bring your inner radiance to the forefront and allow you to get your beauty sleep. Using this meditation technique can rejuvenate your soul, reinvigorate your mind, and restore your body to a place where you can connect with your inner bliss. There is no better time to practice this form of meditation than while lying in bed; you will have an easier time entering a peaceful slumber if you follow this guide.

How to Do It:
1. Lay down in bed and get comfortable. Once you're set, enter a place in your mind where you can disconnect from the outside world.
2. Let go of the stresses and turmoil that have accumulated throughout the day. Even if you had a good day, let go of it. The day is over, and it's time to focus on the peace ahead as you drift off to sleep.
3. Take a deep breath in and slowly breathe out. Pay attention to the way you feel at this moment. Breathe in and out, releasing the tension in your body until you feel the weight of the day has been lifted.
4. Close your eyes and surrender to the calm, loving energy within you. There is a radiance to your soul, so allow it to shine.
5. Remind yourself that you are strong. That you are powerful. That you are beautiful.
6. Accept the peace and renewal that comes with a good night's sleep. Focus on your breathing and let everything else just melt away.
7. Surrender your consciousness to the somnolent reveries of your dreams. You are relaxed and serene, allowing yourself a beautiful night of re-energizing sleep.

Ivy

Ivy Plant.
https://pixabay.com/es/photos/bosque-hiedra-tronco-de-arbol-5159093/

Title: The Survivor
Birthdates: September 30 to October 27
Traits: Determined, Brave, Kind
Compatibility: Ash and Oak

You have a unique personality that can give people pause, but your sharp wit and brilliance usually win them over. Once you become friends with someone, you will cherish them for life. As a dreamer, it can be difficult for you to face reality, but you possess the determination to actually follow through on your more far-fetched goals. During times of struggle, you refuse to complain and press onward with quiet grace. You often turn to spirituality and faith to see you through any difficulties. You are quick to lend your aid to others, sympathizing with their problems due to your own experiences. While you aren't an obvious extrovert, you can be very charismatic when you choose to be, dazzling people with your cleverness and charm.

Exercise to Try: Complete Release Body Scan Meditation

A complete release body scan meditation helps to prepare your mind, body, and spirit to get a healthy amount of sleep. You will make a connection with each part of your body and leave the problems of your waking life behind. This technique can help you evolve your daily meditations to a more effective approach, gaining benefits to a greater extent. Fully scanning your body to ensure a proper release of tension is essential to feeling renewed and at ease when you have finished meditating.

How to Do It:

1. Sit in a chair or lay down in a comfortable position.
2. Take a deep breath in and hold it, then let the breath out. Keep your shoulders steady as you breathe; they shouldn't be going up and down. Slow down your breathing and feel it in your belly. Allow it to expand and contract. Picture a balloon being inflated and deflated each time you inhale and exhale.
3. Be aware of your body, drawing your attention to the sensations within it. Begin at your feet and move upward until you reach your head. As your focus passes across each body part, take note of what you can feel in them. If you feel any soreness or pain, allow yourself to accept it and how you feel about it. Try to breathe through these issues. When you're ready, move along to

the next part of your body.

4. Keep scanning until you've scanned your whole body. Be mindful of any tension you're holding. Often, your neck or back will be some of the primary areas retaining tension. Make a mental note of anywhere with tightness, pressure, or pain. After noticing any discomfort, visualize yourself sending healing energy to those parts of your body. It can be a great method of relieving tension at the moment.

5. Try to recognize the areas where you tend to hold stress. This can be useful even when you're not meditating. Anytime you notice yourself feeling that tension, let your body relax and send a wave of positive energy to release it while controlling your breathing. Always practice mindfulness to make sure you are treating your body with the care it deserves.

Reed

Reed Plant.
https://pixabay.com/es/photos/carrizo-semillas-silvergrass-5110318/

Title: The Inquisitor

Birthdates: October 28 to November 24

Traits: Compassionate, Honest, Curious

Compatibility: Ash and Oak

You are an honorable person with a strong sense of integrity, loathing dishonesty, and disloyalty. Others see you as someone they can confide in since you are easy to talk to about important matters, and they know you can keep a secret. You like to explore deeper into subjects that catch your interest, and your ability to sniff out the truth makes you a natural investigator or journalist. Your curiosity also means you enjoy learning about gossip, scandals, and other hidden stories. Once you reach the truth, you are able to quickly understand the motivation behind it. You also desire to set the record straight since you hate when people are blamed for things they didn't do or weren't involved in.

Exercise to Try: Rainbow Hypnosis Meditation

Rainbow hypnosis meditation is a useful method to help you ease your way into sleep by going through each color of the rainbow. It lets you utilize the power of hypnosis to send your mind into a deep, peaceful state of restfulness. As you take the voyage through the vast ocean of colors, it can enhance the way you dream, ensuring that you will wake up feeling restored and energized.

How to Do It:

1. Lie down flat on your back.
2. Take a deep breath in through your nose, and then let it out through your mouth. Do this three times.
3. Shut your eyes or let your eyelids fall about halfway closed, and choose a focal point for your gaze.
4. Visualize yourself floating on a lake. Imagine the warm, still water surrounding your body and gently carrying you across its surface.
5. Picture yourself looking up at the sky as you float across the water. You feel warm and safe, immersed in the calming waters of the lake. It gently moves you along until you see a rainbow above you.
6. Imagine the rainbow reaching across the sky. It stretches down to the lake, allowing you to float into it. As you move across the rainbow, you can feel the colors wash across your body, relaxing your muscles and infusing you with positive energy.
7. The color red brings you radiant warmth. It feels like standing on a fire that doesn't burn but sends restorative energy from your head to toe. Breathe in and out, allowing yourself to be engulfed by the red energy of the rainbow.
8. The color orange ignites your passion. Allow yourself to think about a subject or activity that brings you joy. Take notice of that

feeling and sustain it, letting you feel that joy deep in your heart. Breathe in and out, infusing your body with the orange energy of the rainbow.

9. The color yellow encourages positivity. Let it expel any negativity from your mind, focusing on the things in your life for which you are thankful. Look for the bright side when thinking about your troubles. Breathe in and out, shining with the light of the yellow energy of the rainbow.

10. The color green bathes you in rejuvenating power. Imagine yourself as a tree, your branches bare as the day's stress has sapped your energy. This restorative power nourishes your roots, and fresh leaves begin to grow until you have been renewed. Breathe in and out, feeding on the green energy of the rainbow.

11. The color blue sparks your creativity. It inspires you to conceive new and exciting ideas, painting a magnificent picture with the palette of your mind. Give yourself permission to dream. Breathe in and out, indulging in your imagination of the blue energy of the rainbow.

12. The color indigo embodies your wisdom. Allow it to give your mind clarity so you can look at any obstacles in your life and make sound decisions about how to deal with them. Use it to remind yourself to consider your experiences and draw forth the lessons they taught you. Breathe in and out, enlightening yourself with the indigo energy of the rainbow.

13. The color purple offers you strength. As it fills your body, it fortifies your muscles, invigorates your spirit, and reinforces your mind. There is no challenge you cannot overcome and no problem that is too difficult for you to solve. Breathe in and out, bolstering your being with the purple energy of the rainbow.

14. As the final color finishes moving through your body, envision the rainbow gently setting you back down into the water. You float all the way back to your bed, coming to rest and feeling the tranquility as a result of your meditation.

Elder

Elder Tree.
https://pixabay.com/es/photos/mayor-planta-%c3%a1rbol-fruta-rama-398009/

Title: The Seeker

Birthdates: November 25 to December 23

Traits: Ambitious, Thoughtful, Loyal

Compatibility: Holly and Alder

You regard your freedom very highly and enjoy being spontaneous. You're a bit of a thrill-seeker, always ready for a good adventure. This zest for life often spreads to others, and they love being around you because of it. There is a big world out there, and you have the ambition to see as much of it as you can. You are also kind and thoughtful, being considerate of other people's feelings and lending assistance when needed. Some people might think that you're shallow or ditzy, but you are actually quite intelligent and philosophical, as your wide range of life experiences has exposed you to many unique perspectives about life.

Exercise to Try: Yoga Nidra Meditation

Yoga Nidra does not focus on relaxation but will still result in you feeling relaxed as a natural side-effect of this meditation technique. It takes you on a journey through every layer of your consciousness until you reach the inner sanctum of your soul. Opening your mind and sweeping away your negative preconceptions and emotions helps you find a more balanced perspective in your life. Self-awareness and self-inquiry allow you to open your heart and find a place for personal acceptance.

How to Do It:

1. Find somewhere with no distractions. This means no noise or visual stimulation. A darkened room or sleep mask will be the best way to block out any light, and if you can't find a quiet place, try earplugs or noise-canceling headphones.

2. Start by lying down on a bed, blanket, or yoga mat, placing a pillow beneath you to support your head, neck, spine, and lower back. Make sure that you're comfortable before you begin meditating.

3. Make sure that your arms are resting on the ground, away from your sides. Your hands should be roughly even with your waist, with your palms facing up. Your legs should also be resting flat on the ground but spread just enough so that your feet line up with your shoulders.

4. Stay completely still and silent. This will aid you in relaxing your mind and body. Slow down your breathing until you are taking gentle breaths without any effort. Close your eyes, allowing your eyelids to rest atop your eyeballs, don't squeeze them shut.

5. Visualize a specific part of your body. It doesn't matter which one; just make sure to focus solely on this body part, avoiding any other distractions. Use your senses to observe what you're feeling in that part of your body. Acknowledge these sensations before moving on to another area.

6. Repeat the previous step until you've gone through every part of your body. Then do the same process for your body as a whole. Envision yourself surrounded by a warm, calming aura. At this point, you should be fully relaxed and relieved of all your tension.

7. Begin to return to an active state. Start by moving your fingers and wiggling them around for a few seconds. Take a deep breath in, hold it for 5 seconds, and then let it out again. Open your eyes and move into a sitting position.

8. Stretch your arms and drop your chin, letting your head hang forward. Roll it from side to side a couple of times. Once you are ready, get to your feet and return to your daily routine.

Chapter 7: Celtic Animal Magic

Celtic Druids and shamans have a strong connection to many types of animals. Their affinity for nature means they view wild creatures and noble beasts as powerful symbolic figures. They often look to the earth, water, and sky for animals to teach them lessons about living in harmony with the environment. In some cases, this reverence for animals evolves into religious worship of them. Some hold a higher position in Celtic society, and certain powers and traits are associated with the most important animals.

Some animals have special significance in Celtic culture.
https://pixabay.com/es/vectors/c%c3%a9ltico-simbolos-animales-gato-40393/

Animals in Celtic Culture

There are many instances of animal symbolism in Celtic art. The illuminated manuscripts created during the medieval era contain beautifully crafted illustrations of creatures representing major religious figures. In the Book of Kells, three of the four authors of the New Testament Gospels are shown as animals significant to Celtic culture - Matthew is depicted as a man, while a lion stands in for Mark, a calf for Luke, and an eagle for John.

The British, Scottish, and Irish aristocracy members include animal symbolism as part of their coat of arms. Many inns and pubs adopt names that include animals, such as the Old Ram in Tivetshall St Mary, the Packhorse and Pig in London, and the Stag's Head in Dublin. Coins minted in Ireland during the 20th century had bulls, wolfhounds, salmon, horses, and Irish hares on their backs. Celtic mythology is rife with instances where people are transformed into wild creatures or animals possessing unique powers that aid their masters in overcoming obstacles.

Animal Symbolism

The animals that have special significance in Celtic culture include the following:

Horses

Horses are considered noble and intelligent creatures, renowned for their speed, endurance, vitality, and beauty. In addition to their revered position in Celtic society, they also had an air of mystery about them. They have a strong connection to the night, particularly in that the term "nightmare" includes "mare," the word for a female horse. This was associated with the goddess Epona, a major figure in Celtic mythology worshiped as the protector of horses and other related creatures.

Besides being one of the most common transportation methods throughout pre-industrialized history, horses were also a regular sight on battlefields. They would carry commanders, archers, and cavalry soldiers, as well as pulling chariots that often gave their riders an advantage in combat. Horse racing was a popular form of entertainment, and many leisure activities included them as a primary component, such as jousting, polo, and fox hunting.

Snakes and Serpents

Despite the well-known myth about St. Patrick driving all the snakes out of Ireland, both snakes and serpents have a long and complicated history with Celtic society. They are said to represent rebirth, creation, and healing. The many winding rivers, streams, and tributaries are described as being serpentine, and snakes are often depicted as a conduit between the spiritual realm and the physical world. Many Celtic symbols, like the triskelion, resemble three coiling serpents.

In Celtic mythology, there is a being known as the Ram-Horned Serpent or Ram-Headed Snake, who often accompanied other gods, particularly in artwork dating from the early Iron Age. The Ram-Horned Serpent was most frequently a companion for Toutatis or Lugh, both chief gods of the religion. There is an association between snakes and the solar wheel, which is evocative of Jörmungandr, the World Serpent from Norse mythology whose entire body encircles the Earth, or Ouroboros from Greek mythology, who is shown eating its own tail and represents the cycle of life, death, and rebirth.

Deer

Deer, especially stags, are connected to Cernunnos, the antlered god of hunting and nature. Does are usually seen as emblematic of birth, renewal, and innocence, while their adult counterparts are associated with virility, abundance, and strength. Antlers are often viewed as a trophy for hunters, and some people can make decent money finding antlers shed by deer in the wild. They are an animal that symbolizes growth in the spring and harvest in the autumn.

White stags appear in Celtic artwork, literature, and mythology. They are said to have come from the Otherworld, and their appearance heralds a period of great transformation that will soon occur. This change can be good or bad, but it is usually an overall positive experience, even if it doesn't seem so at first. Some folklore depicts a person spotting a white stag as presaging a major shift in their fortunes, suddenly gaining a major influx of money and resources.

Dogs and Hounds

As with many cultures, dogs and hounds are considered beloved pets and companions in Celtic society. They remain ever faithful to their masters and never waver in their devotion, loyalty, and love. Dogs are very protective and possess a strong intuition about danger, so keeping them by one's side is always safer than journeying alone. Most dogs will guard their master with their life, and many owners are equally willing to risk their lives for their pets.

Salmon

The ancient Celtic people used salmon as a symbol of knowledge. They represent the accumulation of that knowledge, a vast network of people and experiences that builds over time, all flowing toward the next generation. This is illustrated by the way the rivers, streams, and tributaries where salmon swim all flow to the ocean. Their importance to Celtic culture was so great that the Irish even began minting coins bearing the image of a salmon on its reverse side.

Birds

There is a wide variety of birds that hold significance in Celtic culture. Each type has been assigned its own characteristics, and it would be useful to list them for you now:

- **Ravens**: They are associated with death. Druids often used them in augury, and when flying over a battlefield, they were believed to be a god incarnate.
- **Crows:** They are associated with death, just like ravens. However, crows are generally seen as a negative omen.
- **Cranes:** these represent a false transformation, i.e., claiming you will change when you only superficially alter your actions or behaviors.
- **Peacocks:** They are a symbol of purity.
- **Herons:** are considered ideal for representing loyalty, fidelity, and marriage since they mate for life.
- **Eagles:** skilled hunters with keen eyes, making them an obvious symbol for those who embody similar qualities. They are also considered a noble animal, but one that remains very dangerous.

Finding Your Spirit Animal

Suppose you want to find a spirit animal that can symbolize your personality and character traits. In that case, you can do this in several ways. The most common way involves some soul-searching and careful attention to the details in your life. This process involves the following steps:

- Look to nature and observe the world around you. Watch how different animals behave, how they move, and what they do. The longer you study them, the more familiar you will become with their personalities and the characteristics they embody.

- Learn about your lineage. Depending on who your ancestors were, you might already have a connection to a particular animal without realizing it. Certain animals are very closely linked to a specific culture or group of people.

- Be mindful of your dreams. Your unconscious mind is always making connections that your waking mind doesn't. It can be easy to forget your dreams, so keep a dream journal beside your bed and quickly jot down an entry whenever an animal appears in one of your dreams.

- Keep an eye out for repeat encounters with the same animal. This can be either a real, living animal or just a symbol of it that you find popping up time and time again. There is a good chance that if you notice one type of animal constantly appearing as you go about your day, the universe is trying to tell you something.

- Meditate on the subject. During a meditation session, clear your mind of all thoughts and let your intentions about finding your spirit animal be known. You may discover your thoughts suddenly turn toward a specific animal. This could be your spirit animal guiding you to it.

- Go on a vision quest. Find a shaman willing to lead you through a vision quest to find your spirit animal. This could involve entering a trance-like state, but more often than not, you will only need to follow the shaman's advice on how to find what you seek.

Chapter 8: Earth Magic Rituals

Earth magic is the foundation of all shamanistic wisdom. The power within the earth runs deep, and knowing how to tap into it is a skill most shamans possess. However, you can harness some of the magic contained within the earth for yourself. If you're serious about learning to use earth magic, you must dedicate yourself to practice. It takes a great amount of strength and willpower to wield it properly. If you haven't trained yourself to handle this potent energy, it can end up costing you dearly.

Earth magic is the foundation of all shamanistic wisdom.
Munkhbayar.B, CC BY-SA 4.0 <https://creativecommons.org/licenses/by-sa/4.0>, via Wikimedia Commons:
https://commons.wikimedia.org/wiki/File:Mongol_Darkhad_Shaman_just_starting_Shamanic_ritual.jpg

Earth Magic and Ley Lines

Ley lines are avenues of energy created by the alignment of magically-significant landmarks. These landmarks are set around a location that is infused with energy, and that energy can be directed toward another landmark some distance away. The path linking these connected sites serves as a conduit through which the energy is sent, strengthening the connection between them. Training individuals such as shamans and Druids can tap into the ley lines to help increase the effectiveness of their spells, charms, and rituals.

Celtic Prayers

Here are some prayers that you can recite to help you reinforce your mind, body, and spirit for the purpose of using earth magic:

Prayers to the Earth Mother, Part 1

"Earth Mother

receive in your great bounty

all the blood that has poured over me,

the sorrow that has mired me down.

Let me be free,

so flowers and trees may sprout from me to the heavens,

so birds may come and perch on my wings

and sing their eternal song of gratitude.

Dear Earth Mother,

may your bounty feed the downtrodden,

may you comfort each knee and forehead pressed into your layers,

may la Virgen de Guadalupe's roses flourish

and the trees that become crosses be strong,

may your robes encompass stars, moon, and ocean, day and night,

and hold me in its folds, Earth Mother. O our Mother the Earth, blessed is your name.

Prayer to the Earth Mother, Part 2

"Blessed are your fields and forests, your rocks and mountains, your grasses and trees and flowers, and every green and growing thing.

Blessed are your streams and lakes and rivers, the oceans where our life began, and all your waters that sustain our bodies and refresh our souls.

Blessed is the air we breathe, your atmosphere that surrounds us and binds us to every living thing.

Blessed are all creatures who walk along your surface or swim in your waters or fly through your air, for they are all our relatives.

Blessed are all people who share this planet, for we are all one family, and the same spirit moves through us all.

Blessed is the sun, our day star, bringer of the morning and the heat of summer, giver of light and life.

Blessed is the moon, our night lamp, ruler of the tides, protector of all women, and guardian of our dreams.

Blessed are the stars and planets, the time-keepers, who fill our nights with beauty and our hearts with awe.

O Great Spirit, whose voice we hear in the wind and whose face we see in the morning sun, blessed is your name.

Help us to remember that you are everywhere, and teach us the way of peace."

Prayer to Lugh

"Great, Lugh!
Master of artisans,
leader of craftsmen,
patron of smiths,
I call upon you and honor you this day.
You the many skills and talents,
I ask you to shine upon me and
bless me with your gifts.
Give me strength in skill,

make my hands and mind deft,
and shine light upon my talents.
O mighty Lugh,
I thank you for your blessings."

Prayer to Epona

"Hail Epona Rigantona! Rigantona Epona Hail!
Epona of Horses, I praise you!
Rigantona of the Land, I praise you!
Epona of Sovereignty, I praise you!
Rigantona of Journeys, I praise you!
Epona of Stables, I praise you!
Rigantona of the Otherworld, I praise you!
Epona, Great Mother, I praise you!
Rigantona of the Singing Birds, I praise you!
Epona Rigantona, guide, guardian, and teacher, I praise you!
Epona of Horses, I honor you!
Rigantona of the Land, I honor you!
Epona of Sovereignty, I honor you!
Rigantona of Journeys, I honor you!
Epona of Stables, I honor you!
Rigantona of the Otherworld, I honor you!
Epona, Great Mother, I honor you!
Rigantona of the Singing Birds, I honor you!
Epona Rigantona, guide, guardian, and teacher, I honor you!
Epona of Horses, I thank you for your presence in my life.
Rigantona of the Land, I thank you for the stability in my life.
Epona of Sovereignty, I thank you for the choices you bring to my life.
Rigantona of Journeys, I thank you for your guidance through my life.
Epona of Stables, I thank you for the security in my life.
Rigantona of the Otherworld, I thank you for the mysteries in

my life.

Epona, Great Mother, I thank you for your nurturing presence in my life.

Rigantona of the Singing Birds, I thank you for the beauty you bring to my life.

Epona Rigantona, guide, guardian, and teacher, I thank you for being with me through my life.

Hail Epona Rigantona! Rigantona Epona Hail!"

Creating a Celtic Altar

You can set up a Celtic altar to give yourself a permanent place to practice magic and commune with the gods. The first thing you need to do is decide if you want it to be indoors or outdoors. While having an altar outside will allow you to have a stronger connection to nature, it can be limiting if you live somewhere with frequent inclement weather, especially during the colder part of the year. An indoor altar has the benefit of being accessible at all times. Still, you will have to work harder to forge that connection to nature.

Choose which direction you want your altar to face. Most pagan altars face either north or northeast. Some practitioners of pagan religions that have a Christian influence will face their altars to the east because that's where the sun rises. It's also the traditional direction that many Christian churches are built to face.

Pick a surface or object on which you want to create your altar. This can be anything, from a table to a desk or a piece of furniture. Window sills can also work. If you want, you can even build something from scratch with a few pieces of wood. The important thing is that it has a flat surface and enough room to set up all the components of the altar.

Gather the items and objects you plan to place on your altar. Common options include candles, energy crystals, divination tools, statues or icons of a favored deity, totems of animals, or trinkets with personal significance. At this juncture, you should also decide which colors you want your altar to be. Blue, green, purple, silver, and gold are popular colors, as they often represent the deities and other powers involved in shamanism and Druidry.

When you're ready to set up your altar, get a cloth or cover in the color of your choice and place it over the surface you will use. Now it's time to actually add the items to the altar.

The right side of the altar will be the god's side, where you will place the objects associated with masculine traits. These can be statues or icons of a god, candles with warmer colors like red, orange, yellow, or gold, and totems of male animals, like stags, rams, or lions.

The left side is the goddess' side and will be reserved for objects with feminine traits. These can be statues or icons of a goddess, candles with cooler colors, like green, blue, purple, or silver, and totems of female animals, such as does, ewes, or lionesses.

The middle is where you will place the rest of the objects that are neutral and have no gendered traits. Common items placed in the middle are athames, wands, stones, or a Book of Shadows. After placing the last of the objects, you will be done setting up your altar.

Making a Sacred Space in the Forest

Making a sacred space in the forest is a fairly simple task. All you need is some salt, a small statue, a totem, icon, or picture, and a handful of herbs. Enter the forest and choose a spot with which you feel a connection. Make a rough outline using the salt of the space you want to sanctify. This doesn't need to be very big, just big enough to sit comfortably inside. Crush the herbs up in your hands and scatter them around the space. Finally, place your statue, totem, icon, or picture down within the sanctified area. You can recite prayers and blessings, perform rituals, or cast spells and charms from here. Being so close to nature means you will have an easier time drawing on the earth to aid your magic.

Cleansing and Consecration

If you need to cleanse a location or object, there are some good options to choose from:

- Bury the object in the earth, a bowl of salt, or a sack of cornmeal.
- Burn some incense while walking around the location being cleansed, dispersing its smoke throughout the area.
- Submerge the object in salt water, or fill a spray bottle with salt water and spritz it around the room.

- Purify an object over the flame of a candle, or place it within a fire.
- Fill a bowl or basin with blessed water and let it sit within a location needing cleansing, allowing the negative energy to be drawn into the water (make sure you dispose of the water outside and well away from any homes).
- Use a besom or a blessed broom to sweep away the negative energy.
- If you need to consecrate an item or the ground for performing rituals, you can try these options:
- Using cleansed oils, anoint the items by rubbing the oils across them.
- Consecrate the area using the elements. Perform a ritual involving earth, fire, water, and air. Try lighting a candle, sprinkling some salt, pouring out water, and burning some incense, so the smoke carries into the sky.
- Recite a prayer over the item or ground and make clear your intentions to dedicate the use of the item or space to your chosen deity.

Invoking Awen

Awen is the concept in Welsh mythology that serves as the spark of inspiration and creative energy for poets, bards, and other artists. You can invoke its personification to act as a muse for your artistic endeavors. To invoke Awen, recite the following prayer:

"Hear my words, hear my song
I will sing it to you all day long
Give me a melody, give me a verse
Guide my hand as I rehearse
My heart is heavy as I beg to thee
Draw forth the music, set it free
The wolf howls, the horse neighs
Light the spark that will grow into a blaze
There is power in every word

Don't let this song go unheard
In one voice, we call upon your grace
Take me into your warm embrace
Lose my song like an arrow from a bow
These words are meant for all to know."

Moon Water

You can use moon water in a variety of rituals, spells, and charms. It is a type of blessed water infused with the moon's healing and purification powers. Making it is a very simple process and doesn't take much effort. All you need to do is follow these steps:

1. Choose the type of container you want to use. It should be made of glass so as not to interfere with the moon's energy while also preventing any of its power from escaping. Jars, jugs, or bottles generally work best. If you want to keep out anything from the environment that might fall into the water, use a container with a secure lid.

2. Fill the container with water. Fresh rainwater is preferable since it's natural and pure. Tap water is usually run through a treatment plant, so it can be contaminated with undesirable chemicals and pollutants. However, if you would like to drink your moon water, use bottled spring water.

3. Place your container of water in direct moonlight. This can be either inside or outside, as long as there aren't any obstructions between your water and the moon.

4. Recite a prayer over the water. It doesn't need to be anything too extensive. Something simple like, "Goddess of the moon, bless this water with your radiant light."

5. Place a crystal on top of the container to amplify the energy infusing the water. Amethyst, citrine, clear quartz, or moonstone are all great choices.

6. Leave the container sitting in the moonlight overnight. Let it soak under the moon for several nights for stronger moon water. Once you're satisfied that you've let it charge with enough energy, your moon water will be ready to use.

Sacred Trees and Plants

Here is a list of the sacred trees and plants important to Celtic earth magic:

Alder
Alder is a deciduous tree with serrated leaves and bearing catkins. It is believed to be able to hide and protect people from danger. The traits associated with it are protection, strength, confidence, and determination.

Apple
Apple trees are considered sacred in many cultures. It gets its name from the fruit it bears. The traits associated with it are good health and happiness.

Ash
Ash is noted for having hardwood with a straight grain. It is considered a symbol of power, sturdiness, and immortality. If you place leaves from an ash tree beneath your pillow, it is said to stimulate prophetic dreams.

Birch
Birch is a thin-leaved hardwood tree whose bark was used by heroic figures in Celtic mythology to write messages using Ogham. It symbolizes rebirth, growth, and new beginnings.

Blackthorn
Blackthorn is a winter tree. It has white flowers that grow before the leaves come in during the spring. Unfortunately, it has a poor reputation, as it represents black magic and the Crone facet of the Triple Goddess.

Broom
Broom is a shrub whose flowers can be used to make yellow dye. It represents healing and royalty, as it was the official emblem of Geoffrey of Anjou, father of the English king Henry II.

Cedar
Cedar trees have evergreen leaves and wood that carry a distinctive scent. It was popular with the Celtic people from Continental Europe, who used its oil as a preservative. It symbolizes nobility, strength, and greatness.

Elder
Elder plants, also known as elderberries, were used by the ancient Celtic people in cooking recipes, spells, rituals, and festival celebrations. It is believed that they would rub the juices from the elderberries on their cheeks to make them look redder, similar to how someone would use rouge today.

Elm
Elm is a tree with slightly fibrous, tan-colored wood that has a slight sheen. It is closely associated with the Otherworld, and many of the forests in the British Isles are made up mainly of elms. The wood from these trees has an interlocking grain that makes it highly resistant to splitting, causing it to be greatly valued for use in constructing items that need to be very strong.

Fir
Fir trees are tall and slender evergreens with needles and cones that resemble those of pines. They represent unity, family, and kindness, often being used as Christmas trees.

Hawthorn
Hawthorn is a shrub or small tree also known as hawberry and Mayflower. It symbolizes love and protection, and its berries have been used in love spells and marriage ceremonies. The dried fruits of hawthorn have medicinal properties, being used in some places around the world as a digestive aid.

Oak
Oak trees were considered sacred by the Celtic people since their size and longevity lent them to be a constant presence within a community, even as generation after generation of people passed on. It has a solid, sturdy, dense wood that can be used in many construction projects, especially as building frames and support beams. The traits associated with it are strength, longevity, stability, endurance, honesty, power, and justice.

Pine
Pine is an evergreen tree with fragrant needles and pine cones. It represents fertility, regeneration, and immortality. Their wood is the most commonly used type of timber for commercial purposes.

Rowan

Rowan is also known as mountain ash and has a dense wood perfect for carving sculptures and other works of art. It symbolizes wisdom, knowledge, and protection, and the Celtic people believed it could be used to ward off evil spirits and malevolent forces. Druids view rowan as a threshold between the physical world and the Otherworld.

Silver Fir

Silver fir is a tall, evergreen coniferous tree with a surprisingly strong, lightweight, even-textured wood with a fine grain. It is typically used in constructing furniture and paper, while its oil is present in perfumes and other aromatic products. The traits associated with it include hope, courage, and good fortune.

Willow

Willow trees have elongated leaves that hang down from their branches and can often be seen swaying in the wind. They symbolize adaptability, flexibility, and healing. Interestingly, chewing on the bark of a willow tree is believed to offer some relief from pain.

Yew

Yew is a coniferous tree that grows slowly but lives a very long time. It is associated with the Winter Solstice, death, and rebirth. The ancient Celtic people used the wood from yew trees to make a wide variety of weapons, tools, and other objects.

Chapter 9: Celtic Spells and Charms

Celtic magic is a tradition that goes back as far as the culture itself. Shamans and Druids both practiced forms of magic, and it was not uncommon for certain community members who had an affinity for spells and charms to take up the role of a local witch. Unlike the modern depictions of such people, most users of magic in the ancient Celtic society were viewed as wise, and their assistance with advice and abilities as healers made them valued members of the community. While much of the actual magic practiced by the ancient Celts has been lost to time, bits and pieces have been preserved by families who possess their own Book of Shadows.

Most Books of Shadows are unique, as the owners curate the specific collection of texts within it.
https://pixabay.com/es/photos/libro-naturaleza-sombra-leyendo-2669150/

Book of Shadows

The Book of Shadows is a corpus found within neopagan religions that contains religious texts and instructions on performing magical spells, charms, and rituals. It is traditionally passed down from one generation to the next within the same family, making it akin to the custom of a family Bible kept by many Christians. Most Books of Shadows are unique, as the specific collection of texts within it is curated by the owners, adding additional pieces to it as they learn new spells, charms, and rituals. Some families will also include personal writings that shine a light on their own journey through life as a neopagan practitioner.

One thing to remember about neopagan magic is the "Rule of Three," or the "Threefold Law." This asserts that any energy you put out in the world will return to you threefold, or three times as much as you put out. The intent of magical spells, charms, and rituals is to put out positive energy, so the positive energy that returns to you will be magnified by three. You must never attempt to use magic that puts out negative energy. Whatever short-term benefits it might grant you, the negative energy that returns will cause consequences that far outweigh whatever you might have gained.

Celtic Spells

Here is a list of different spells you can try on your own:

Spell for Good Fortune

This spell is meant to provide you with good luck. You will need the following:

- A candle
- String
- A trinket

Light the candle, then loop the string through the trinket and tie it. Start swinging the trinket above the flame and chant:

"A candle flickers, this trinket I pass, good energy and fortune come to me, wealth, knowledge, influence, energy. By good means come to me, wealth, knowledge, influence, energy. This trinket I pass into power, to attract to me wealth, knowledge, influence, energy, come to me!"

Repeat this three times, then wear the "necklace" around your neck. The more you do this, the more powerful the effect will be."

Beauty Spell

This spell is meant to increase your attractiveness. You will need the following:

- A mirror
- A camera
- A candle

To cast it, you must do the following:

During a full moon, take a mirror and go outside. If you can't go outside, just open a window and ensure the moon is reflected in the mirror.

Take a picture of your hair, lips, eyes, or whatever you want to change, and place it on the mirror.

While concentrating on it, say, *"Moonshine, Starlight, let the wind carry your light. Let your glow cover my body, and let your shine cover every eye."*

Once you are done, dispose of the picture by burning it with a candle. Repeat these steps to improve the effects of the spell."

Dragon's Blood Peace Spell

This spell is meant to keep the peace within your home. You will need the following:

- A glass bottle, flask, or vial
- Red, flexible sealing wax
- Matches or a lighter
- Sugar
- Salt
- Dragon's Blood Powder (a powdered form of a resin extracted from the fruit of the Calamus Draco tree)

First, mix together the ingredients, adding 1 part sugar, 1 part salt, and 1 part Dragon's blood.

Seal the bottle, flask, or vial with the red wax.

Recite the following spell: *"I call upon the Mother of Earth to grant me peace.*

I ask you to bless this home with serenity.

Let clear minds overcome angry hearts.

Let gentleness and kindness infuse this space."

Place the sealed container in a shared space around your home where your family spends a significant amount of time, such as the kitchen or a living room. This spell will give off a calming energy and keep the peace between your family members."

Celtic Charms

Here's a list of charms you can try on your own:

Protection Charm

A standard protection charm will create a field of energy surrounding your chosen space. The larger the area, the more energy is needed to keep them active. To cast this charm, you will need the following:

- 3-5 candles
- A doll or effigy
- Chamomile petals
- Pen and paper
- Matches or lighter
- Flame-resistant bowl or ashtray

Starting off, write the following down on the piece of paper, "Please protect this space from all harm. I trust in the power of the gods and goddesses, and I will not allow negative energy to invade my space. Once this charm has been cast, it will protect this space for three times three days."

When you have finished writing, fold the paper up and place it in the bowl or ashtray. Now you must set the candles up around the perimeter of the area that you wish to protect. This can be in the shape of a triangle, square, rectangle, circle, or five-point star.

After you set the candle down, light it and say the following: *"I light this flame to ward off any evil that seeks to invade my space. So long as it burns, no darkness will seep through its barrier."*

Repeat this for each candle, and then return to the bowl with the paper in it. Place the doll or effigy in front of it. This will represent the power of the charm, as you will channel the protective energy into it. Sprinkle the chamomile petals into the bowl over it, and then set the paper aflame.

As it burns, focus on visualizing a protective layer of energy surrounding your chosen area. Hold your doll or effigy in your hand when the flames have died down and speak these words: "This power now protects my space from all harm. *I have nothing to fear from anything outside it. Thank you for delivering me from the darkness and into the light.*"

It is now safe to snuff out the candles, as the protection charm is fueled by the energy you put into the doll or effigy. It must remain within the protected area in order to work. Taking it beyond the perimeter you've established will cause it to lose its effect and leave you vulnerable to harm. After nine days, you can burn or bury the doll or effigy, as its power has been spent. You can repeat the charm ritual if you desire to maintain the protection magic keeping you safe."

Charm against Depression

Depression is sometimes known as a "Fairy Blast," as the ancient Celts believed that when a person fell into a listless, unenergetic, emotionally-numb state, they were no longer themselves. A fairy was said to have been the culprit, and a Fairy Doctor was brought in to counter the negative effects of the Fairy Blast. You can cast the same charm that they did to rid the afflicted person of the Fairy Blast. To do this, you will need the following:

- Blessed water
- A basin
- Fire (a candle or hearth)
- Incense sticks

Before you begin, light the candle or hearth. You first need to pour the blessed water over the person's hands, catching it in the basin.

As you do this, say: *"In the name of Lugh, who shows strength before the gods and stands among them, lend me your shining sword so that I might rid this poor soul of their afflictions."*

Be careful to avoid letting the water get sullied. Next, light the incense sticks and hold them in front of the person. Allow them to burn for several minutes, infusing the air with its protective energy.

Once you have finished burning the sticks, say: *"Cast off this veil and return this person to me. Begone, fairies! I know you for what you are. Begone from this place!"*

Place the candle and incense sticks into the basin with the water to put them out, or toss the water over the fire in your hearth. This charm will help ward off any further symptoms of depression."

Creating Your Own Book of Shadows

You can create your own Book of Shadows by copying these spells and charms with handwriting onto a piece of paper. Do not just print them off, as the texts within your Book of Shadows should all have a personal touch. Add in any notes from your experience with attempting the spells and charms. You can also write up a brief summary of what first got you interested in Celtic magic and the first steps you took to learn about it. Although your Book of Shadows will be relatively thin initially, as you add more to it over the years, you will gather an impressive amount of knowledge that you can then pass on to the next generation in your family.

Chapter 10: Celtic Holidays and Festivals

Many Celtic holidays and festivals throughout the calendar year celebrate various aspects of Celtic society. The main festivals are those from the Wheel of the Year. Still, plenty of minor holidays focus on more niche subjects, such as a feast dedicated to a single deity or a seasonal occasion. The Celtic people loved to celebrate. Their festivals often included singing, dancing, music, games, feasts, bonfires, rituals, and dedications to the gods.

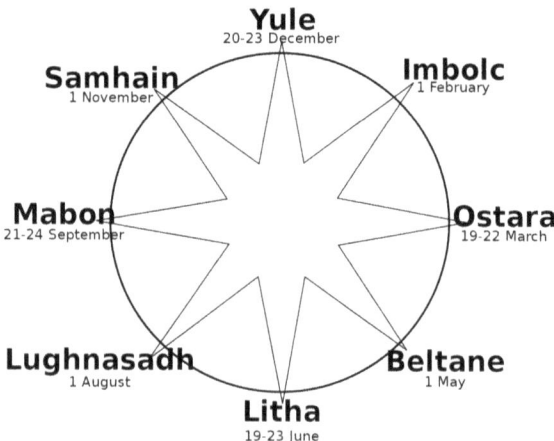

Many Celtic holidays and festivals throughout the calendar year celebrate various aspects of Celtic society.
https://commons.wikimedia.org/wiki/File:Wheel_of_the_Year.svg

The Wheel of the Year

The Wheel of the Year is a cycle of eight annual seasonal festivals that coincide with major solar events, such as the solstices and equinoxes and the midpoints between them. These eight festivals can be laid out around the Wheel of the Year, turning it as the seasons come and go, with the current solar event or midpoint sitting at the top. Just as each calendar year involves a cycle of seasons associated with birth, growth, maturity, death, and rebirth, all things within the world experience a similar cycle.

Imbolc

Imbolc is the festival celebrated halfway between the winter solstice and the vernal equinox. It marks the beginning of spring when the land is going through the birth and rebirth part of the cycle. This is when seeds are starting to be sown, and spring cleaning is a common tradition. The Celtic people would visit holy wells, praying for good health. They would recite these prayers while walking "sunwise," or clockwise, around the well. Offerings of coins or "clooties" were often left for the gods, and water drawn from the wells was used in cleansings and blessings of the home, livestock, crop fields, and loved ones.

The Celtic pagans dedicated Imbolc to the goddess Brigid, syncretized with St. Brigid by the Christian Church, adopting this festival as St. Brigid's Day. People would leave strips of cloth or clothing outside, hoping that St. Brigid would bless them. Christians also celebrate this day as Candlemas, which commemorates the presentation of Jesus at the Temple. Imbolc is the first of the three spring festivals. In Wales, this festival is called "Gŵyl Fair y Canhwyllau," which translates to "Mary's Festival of the Candles."

Ostara

Ostara is a festival that falls on the vernal equinox. This day has roughly the same amount of day and night, balancing darkness and light. However, it marks the point when day will start to overtake night, with light on the rise. Nature is in full bloom, with many plants flowering and new animals entering their major growth stage. The Christian liturgical calendar uses the vernal equinox to determine when Easter will be celebrated yearly since it is a moveable feast with no set date. Ostara is the second of the three spring festivals. In Wales, this festival is called "Alban Eilir," which translates to "Equinox of the Spring."

Beltane

Beltane is the festival celebrated halfway between the vernal equinox and summer solstice. It marks the end of spring and the beginning of summer when the land is going through the growth part of the cycle. It is also known as May Day, and maypoles are a popular tradition for the Celtic people and the cultures descended from them. Bonfires are another typical activity for celebrating this festival. In the past, sacrifices occurred alongside the bonfires, but these practices have been phased out by the neopagans and modern cultures.

Certain traditions, such as warding off or appeasing the fairies in an effort to protect crops and livestock, are still practiced today. Like with Imbolc, holy wells are visited, moving sunwise around them, and similar offerings are left to receive a blessing from the gods. Traditional foods are prepared, and feasts are given for families and communities to celebrate together, sharing in one's good fortune and asking for blessings and protection during the oncoming season. Beltane is the third of the three spring festivals. In Wales, this festival is called "Calan Haf," which translates to "First Day of Summer."

Litha

Litha is the festival that falls on the summer solstice, the longest day of the year, and as the midpoint of the season, it is also known as Midsummer. Nature is at the peak of its maturation, reaching the end of the growth part of the cycle. Much of this festival consists of venerating the sun, giving it thanks for its nourishing light, and asking the gods to protect their crops and livestock until the harvest season. Some celebrations go on late into the night, with candles and bonfires preserving the light through the shortest period of darkness for the year. Dancing, singing, feasting, and other revelries often occur during this holiday. Litha is the only summer festival. In Wales, this festival is called "Alban Hefin," which translates to "Solstice of the Summer."

Lughnasadh

Lughnasadh is the festival celebrated halfway between the summer solstice and the autumnal equinox. It marks the start of the harvest season, as well as the end of summer and the beginning of autumn. One of the most popular traditions during this festival is baking bread using the first grains harvested that year. Some people also bake a small figure representing the god Lugh into their bread, believing this will ensure a bountiful harvest that season.

Christianity syncretized their harvest festival with Lughnasadh, known as Lammas, or the Loaf Mass Day. Their customs are similar to that of the pagan holiday, including baking bread with the first harvested grains. However, rather than offerings to the pagan gods, Christians give thanks and pray to the Abrahamic God and Jesus Christ. They also celebrate the feast of St. Alphonsus Liguori on this day, which coincides with the date of his death. Lughnasadh is the first of the three autumn or harvest festivals. In Wales, this festival is called "Calan Awst," which translates to "First Day of August."

Mabon

Mabon is the festival that falls on the autumnal equinox. This day has roughly the same amount of night and day, balancing darkness and light. However, it marks the point when night will start to overtake day, with darkness on the rise. This is when crops have reached their full maturity and are waiting to be reaped. Neopagans perform a thanksgiving ritual, showing gratitude for the fruits yielded by the earth and recognizing their duty to share their good fortune with others. They also seek to gain the gods' blessing for the oncoming winter. Mabon is the second of the autumn or harvest festivals. Its name is actually derived from the figure of Mabon ap Modron in Welsh mythology, but it is also known in Wales as "Alban Elfed," which translates to "Equinox of the Autumn."

Samhain

Samhain is the festival celebrated halfway between the autumnal equinox and winter solstice. It marks the end of summer and the beginning of winter – when the land is going through the death part of the cycle. The name Samhain is Gaelic for "Summer's End." The harvest season ends when the crops have yielded up the last of their bounty. The Celtic people would have bonfires and perform divination rituals during this time, as it was customary to honor the dead and appease the spirits. It was believed that the veil between the physical world and the spiritual realm was at its weakest during Samhain, allowing the spirits to walk the Earth for the duration of the festival.

There was a popular tradition known as *mumming and guising*, where people dressed in costume or disguise, wearing masks or painting their faces. The idea was that they would be impersonating the spirits and souls of the dead, protecting them from harm by blending in with these supernatural entities. They went door to door, singing songs and reciting verses in exchange for food or treats. The mummers would threaten that they would do mischief to the residents if they were not compensated for their efforts.

The practice of mumming and guising is very similar to the modern custom of "trick or treating," where people (usually children) dress up in costumes and visit houses to get candy or treats. The name of the activity harkens back to the older Celtic tradition, where the rhetorical choice of a "trick" or a "treat" is similar to the threat of doing mischief if the mummer was not given food. Trick or treating normally takes place on Halloween, or All Hallows' Eve, which is the eve of the Christian holiday known as All Hallows' Day or All Saints' Day. This is another instance of syncretization, with the Christian Church adopting Samhain and some of its traditions for their own holiday. Samhain is the third of the autumn or harvest festivals. In Wales, this festival is called "Nos Calan Gaeaf," which translates to "Eve of the First Day of Winter."

Yule

Yule is the festival that falls on the winter solstice. This is the shortest day of the year, and as it is the midpoint of the winter season, it is also called Midwinter. Nature is at the nadir of the death part of the cycle but preparing to enter the rebirth part. Christianity syncretized Yule with their midwinter holidays, resulting in the liturgical season known as Christmastide. Gift-giving and feasting are popular customs for this festival, as well as having gatherings of friends and family. A Yule log is traditionally chosen and burnt in the hearth, and the warmth and light are meant to protect the home from the harsh, wintry conditions outside. Yule is the only winter festival. In Wales, this festival is called "Alban Arthan," which translates to "Solstice of the Little Bear," a name that refers to the Welsh myths of King Arthur.

Appendix: Glossary of Gaelic Terms

Celt/Celtic: A collection of Indo-European people connected by their shared cultural experiences and languages.

Gael/Gaelic: The native peoples from Ireland, Scotland, and the Isle of Man. They speak a branch of the Celtic languages known as Gaelic (Irish), Scottish Gaelic, and Manx.

Shaman: A religious figure who can access the spiritual realm and influence good and evil spirits. They enter a trance-like state during rituals and ceremonies and practice healing and divination.

Druid: A high-ranking member within ancient Celtic society who served as a religious leader, keeper of lore; also, legal authorities, adjudicators, healers, and political advisors. Modern Druids serve a similar function, although they now mostly focus on the religious, historical, and healing aspects of their role.

Spiritual Realm: Also known as the Spirit Realm, it is a hidden world that exists alongside the physical world but is unable to be accessed by most people. This is where many spirits dwell, and shamans are proficient in communicating with spirits across the veil and entering the spiritual realm through ritualistic means.

Otherworld: A realm of deities and supernatural beings that features heavily in Celtic, Irish, and Welsh mythology. It is also where the souls of the dead go after their physical body perishes.

Soul: The immaterial essence and energy of a human being that exists separate from their physical body.

Spirit: The soul of a person, animal, or other creature, as well as certain supernatural beings that lack a physical body.

Animism: The belief that plants, inanimate objects, and other natural phenomena have a living spirit.

Entheogens: Any chemical substance, usually coming from an organic source, which can be ingested to produce an altered state of consciousness for religious or spiritual purposes. Shamans normally use these to enter a trance in order to commune with spirits or enter the spiritual realm.

Ogham: An ancient Celtic alphabet consisting of 25 (originally 20) characters that are formed by parallel tally marks, dashes, dots, or other basic shapes in various configurations across a continuous line.

Tree Astrology: A practice of predicting a person's personality and specific traits based on their date of birth and when during a season this occurred. Each category is based on the movement of the moon coordinated with a lunar calendar that results in 13 signs instead of the 12 in the zodiac.

Awen: A concept from Welsh mythology defined as a creative energy that inspires poets, bards, and other artists. It can also be the personification of a muse for creative artists in general.

The Wheel of the Year: The annual cycle of seasonal festivals, consisting of the year's primary solar events (the solstices and equinoxes) and the midpoints between them.

Imbolc: The festival is halfway between the winter solstice and the vernal equinox that marks the beginning of spring and is also known as Candlemas.

Ostara: The festival that falls on the vernal equinox when there is a balance between darkness and light, with light on the rise.

Beltane: The festival is halfway between the vernal equinox and summer solstice that marks the beginning of summer, and is also known as May Day.

Litha: The festival that falls on the summer solstice, also known as Midsummer, is the longest day of the year.

Lughnasadh: The festival is halfway between the summer solstice and the autumnal equinox; it marks the start of the harvest season and is also known as Lammas.

Mabon: The festival that falls on the autumnal equinox when there is a balance between light and darkness, with darkness on the rise.

Samhain: The festival is halfway between the autumnal equinox and winter solstice, marking the end of the harvest season, and is also known as Halloween.

Yule: The festival that falls on the winter solstice, also known as Christmastide, is the shortest day of the year.

Here's another book by Silvia Hill that you might like

Free Bonus from Silvia Hill available for limited time

Hi Spirituality Lovers!

My name is Silvia Hill, and first off, I want to THANK YOU for reading my book.

Now you have a chance to join my exclusive spirituality email list so you can get the ebooks below for free as well as the potential to get more spirituality ebooks for free! Simply click the link below to join.

P.S. Remember that it's 100% free to join the list.

$27 FREE BONUSES

9 Types of Spirit Guides and How to Connect to Them

How to Develop Your Intuition: 7 Secrets for Psychic Development and Tarot Reading

Tarot Reading Secrets for Love, Career, and General Messages

Access your free bonuses here
https://livetolearn.lpages.co/celtic-shamanism-paperback/

References

Berry, L. A. (2022, August 25). Who were the Druids? A history of Druidism in Britain. British Heritage. https://britishheritage.com/history/history-Druids-britain

Burrows, G. (2020). Portico: The near future thriller that will keep you guessing. Gideon Burrows. https://access.portico.org/Portico/auView?auId=ark:%2F27927%2Fphzjqstqh

Caesar, G. J. (2017). Bellum Gallicum (J. H. Schmalz, Ed.). de Gruyter Mouton.

Carney, J. (1975). The Invention of the Ogam Cipher. Ériu, 22, 62–63.

Cox, R. A. V. (1999). The language of the ogam inscriptions of Scotland. An Clo Gaidhealach.

Cross, T. P., & Slover, C. H. (1995). Ancient Irish tales: The ulster cycle. Four Courts Press.

Curriculum Development Unit. (1982). Heroic tales from the ulster cycle (2nd ed.). O'Brien Press.

Dan. (2012, November 15). Shamanism. Norse Mythology for Smart People. https://norse-mythology.org/concepts/shamanism/

Davis, R. E., Peterson, K. E., Rothschild, S. K., & Resnicow, K. (2011). Pushing the envelope for cultural appropriateness: does evidence support cultural tailoring in type 2 diabetes interventions for Mexican American adults? The Diabetes Educator, 37(2), 227–238. https://doi.org/10.1177/0145721710395329

Eickhoff, R. L. (2004). The Red Branch tales: The sixth book in the ulster cycle. Forge.

Fhearaigh, C., & Stampton, T. (1998). Ogham: An Irish alphabet. Hippocrene Books.

Glosecki, S. O. (1988). Wolf of the bees: Germanic shamanism and the bear hero. Journal of Ritual Studies, 2(1), 31–53. http://www.jstor.org/stable/44368362

Harris, K. (n.d.). Mythology: Oak trees and why people worshiped them. History Daily. https://historydaily.org/tree-gods-worshiping-mighty-oak-trees/8

Info. (2020a, February 11). A re-evaluation of the ogham tree list. Order of Bards, Ovates & Druids. https://Druidry.org/resources/a-re-evaluation-of-the-ogham-tree-list

Info. (2020b, February 11). Anglo-Celtic medicine ways - the shamanism of pre-Christian Britain. Order of Bards, Ovates & Druids. https://Druidry.org/resources/anglo-celtic-medicine-ways-the-shamanism-of-pre-christian-britain

Jackson, K. (1948). A Grammar of Old Irish. R. Thurneysen, D. A. Binchy, Osborn Bergin. Speculum, 23(2), 335–339. https://doi.org/10.2307/2852977

Loh-Hagan, V. (2020). Celtic tree astrology. 45th Parallel Press.

MacManus, S. (1988). Rocky road to Dublin. Moytura Press.

MacNeill, E. (1931). Archaisms in the Ogham Inscriptions. Hodges Figgis.

Martin, G. R. R. (2011). Song of ice and fire set: A game of thrones, a clash of kings, a storm of swords, a feast for crows, a dance with dragons. Zatpix Re-Packaged Edition.

Miller, M. (2012). Ogham - the magical Celtic tree alphabet (2nd ed.). Ogma Publications.

Moss, V. (1985). Beating the stress connection. Self-hypnosis. AORN Journal, 41(4), 720–722.

Ogham translator - online ogam writing converter. (n.d.). Dcode.Fr https://www.dcode.fr/ogham-alphabet

O'Hara, K. (2022, January 10). 15 Celtic symbols and meanings (an Irishman's 2022 guide). The Irish Road Trip. https://www.theirishroadtrip.com/celtic-symbols-and-meanings/

Padilla, R., Gomez, V., Biggerstaff, S. L., & Mehler, P. S. (2001). Use of curanderismo in a public health care system. Archives of Internal Medicine, 161(10), 1336–1340. https://doi.org/10.1001/archinte.161.10.1336

Piattelli-Palmarini, M. (2000). Tower of babel. Trends in Ecology & Evolution, 15(4), 173–174. https://doi.org/10.1016/s0169-5347(99)01804-2

Reyes-Ortiz, C. A., Rodriguez, M., & Markides, K. S. (2009). The role of spirituality healing with perceptions of the medical encounter among Latinos. Journal of General Internal Medicine, 24 Suppl 3(S3), 542–547.

https://doi.org/10.1007/s11606-009-1067-9

Ryan, C. (2012). Border states in the work of Tom Mac Intyre: A Paleo-postmodern perspective. Cambridge Scholars Publishing.

Salter, A. (1941). Three Techniques of Autohypnosis. The Journal of General Psychology, 24(2), 423–438. https://doi.org/10.1080/00221309.1941.10544386

Sinn, S. (2011, July 13). Muin (grape vine). Living Library. https://livinglibraryblog.com/muin-grape/

Skjalden. (2018, March 11). Völva the viking witch or seeress. Nordic Culture. https://skjalden.com/volva-the-viking-witch-or-seeress/

Sleath, B. L., & Williams, J. W., Jr. (2004). Hispanic ethnicity, language, and depression: physician-patient communication and patient use of alternative treatments. International Journal of Psychiatry in Medicine, 34(3), 235–246. https://doi.org/10.2190/VQU1-QYWT-XW6Y-4M14

Spence, L. (2005). Celtic spells and charms. Kessinger Publishing.

Spilsbury, L. (2017). The Mayas. Raintree.

Stewart Macalister, R. A. (2014). The secret languages of Ireland. Cambridge University Press.

Terravara. (2021, April 23). Shamanism vs Druidism: What's the difference? Terravara. https://www.terravara.com/shamanism-vs-Druidism/

The origins of shamanism. (n.d.). Gaia. https://www.gaia.com/article/how-much-do-you-know-about-shamanism

Walsh, J. K. (2017). Tezcatlipoca, the Smoking Mirror. Createspace Independent Publishing Platform.

Williams, B. (1996). The Roman conquest of Britain. Heinemann Library.

Williams, T. W. (2013). In quest of life; Or, the revelations of the wiyatatao of xipantl. The last high priest of the Aztecs. Theclassics

Milton Keynes UK
Ingram Content Group UK Ltd.
UKHW020624111124
2732UKWH00004B/12